Who's *in your* Top Hive?

your guide
to finding your
success
mentors

Bert Gervais

Who's in Your Top Hive:
Your Guide To Finding Your Success Mentors.
Copyright © 2010 by Bertrand Gervais

ISBN 978-0-615-36875-7

Published 2010
Printed by Success Press Publishing in the United States of America

Graphic Design & Layout:
Raheel Ahmed - Emage Graphic Studio.

:: Acknowledgments

I never thought that ideas on scrap paper could become a book. This is a dream come true for me! Without the help of key friends, family, and relatives, none of this would be possible. I would first like to thank G-d. In my darkest hours you have always stood by me.

To my brother, Patrice Gervais, for putting up with a knucklehead little brother for so many years. My best qualities are yours. To this day you still remind me that you inherited the looks in the family. I decided to put our baby pictures here so that the readers can judge for themselves. (I'm the one on the right.)

To my mother, Marie Laura, and my father, Pierre-Richard, for keeping me grounded in hard work and humility. You worked tirelessly to raise me right and deserve the credit for much that is right with me, and you can't be held responsible for my shortcomings.

To Arel Moodie. Can anyone ask for a better best friend? Thank you for never accepting anything less than the best from me! To Professor Angelo Mastrangelo, my first mentor, for saving my life. Without you my life would have been far different. Thank you for helping me to think more deeply about my purpose. To Dan Demaionewton for pushing me to think bigger about my purpose.

To Alain Antoine and Fred Lherisson for showing me how to put family first.

To Ayumi Nagano and Chris Jackson for giving up part of your Thanksgiving to visit me in the hospital and make me laugh.

To John Hinds. This book would not be possible without you. Without your mentorship, these words wouldn't exist. Especially to Monica Perry, who sparked my love of mentorship during my days as a Gear Up mentor.

To my cousins, aunts, and uncles, for their love and support throughout the years.

To Regine and Norman Bowen for their guidance and belief in my ability. To Rudy Racine for your invaluable guidance, and for always challenging me to be excellent.

To Michael Simmons and Sheena Lindahl for mentoring me and helping me to grow professionally. To Winston Thompson and Rotimi Paul for your positive cheer and support. To Patricia Hudak for your support, accountability, and refusal to let me fail.

To everyone who has mentored me and helped me along the way including Bea Fields, Andrew Morrison, Stacie Grant, Gil Pessoa, Mrs. Gould, Professor Francis Battisti, and especially Marlene Green. Marlene, you opened so many doors for me and believed in me at a time when I badly needed support.

To Dave Lichey. If I had only been smart enough to listen to you back then. Please know that I always valued your friendship and your guidance.

To everyone who helped to make this book possible including Tania Gomez, my graphic design team at Enki Communications, my editors Lindsey Donner and Tanya Arditi. To Laurie Davis, Dweynie Paul and many others. To Professor Anthony Mayo for believing in my cause.

:: **Table of** Contents

:: What This Book
Will Do For You

Every chapter of this book contains dozens of proven, practical ideas that will help you gain the success, happiness, and career satisfaction you so desperately want. These ideas are brought to life by real success stories of real people just like you. If you apply just one idea you learn here, then reading this book is worth your time.

I don't want you to read this book and say, "Wow, that was great book. I feel so pumped about my future that I'm gonna go lie down, eat some soft-baked cookies, and play Nintendo Wii!"

What will that do for you? Instead, I want you to finish this book and say, "Wow, that was an amazing book. I'm going to take action...on one idea...right now...today!"

By the time you finish reading every single word of this book, you will understand:

➢ The secret to a deeply satisfying and successful career

➢ Where to find great mentors and what to say when you meet them

➢ Three tips for winning the confidence of your mentors

➢ The key phrase to turn a skeptical mentor into an enthusiastic supporter

➢ The four types of mentor relationships that all successful people have

Chapter One:

Introduction

I didn't become successful because I climbed on the backs of people around me. I became successful because those people lifted me up.

-Russell Simmons

Chapter One

Why is it that some people can accomplish in five years what it takes others 10 years to achieve? When you look at top achievers, from Mark Zuckerberg of Facebook, to Oprah Winfrey, to President Barack Obama, you find one common thread: their attitude and their ability to work with mentors. These achievers all tapped into the benefits of mentorship: priceless perspective, know-how, and the emotional confidence to release your inner genius. Your ability to accelerate your success and elevate yourself above your peers hinges upon your attitude towards those around you.

You've heard all of this before: promises that connections are all it takes to make it. But why step out of your comfort zone to find meaningful relationships at work? Why find a mentor and learn under their wing? All just to get ahead? It seems so outdated. Can't you just pave your own way like the Michael Dells and Gordon Gekkos of the world?

All around you there are people who have unique knowledge, experience, and expertise that can greatly benefit you. Sadly, some of us will never meet these people. Some of us will never experience the life-changing power of making these meaningful connections, and we effectively lose out on the opportunity to finally take charge of our lives and careers. But that doesn't have to be you.

This book is about finding those mentors who are the right fit for you, mentors who can support your growth and help you achieve your dreams. Oprah once famously said that a mentor is "someone who allows you to see hope inside of yourself." Her fourth grade teacher, Mrs. Duncan, gave her that hope, and a love for words, at an early age. The man who invented the personal computer, Ed Roberts, mentored then 20-year-old Bill Gates and allowed him the rare opportunity to code software for personal computers. That experience and Robert's advice helped him to launch Microsoft.

Who will be that person for you?

I know what you're thinking. You're wondering, how can I join the few lucky folks who seem to snatch up all the good mentors?

The good news is that finding the right mentor has nothing to do with chance or luck. We all have attitudes and beliefs that are either magnetic or repellent to the people around us. Every single day, we are either attracting or pushing away the type of person who could launch us to another level of success, if only we let them.

There has never been a more important time to stand apart from the crowd.

We live in a rapidly changing and uncertain world. For the first time in American history we have four generations working side by side in the workplace. As boomers get set to retire, companies are looking to recent college graduates for the next class of hungry go-getters to move up. That's you, right? Good, because the opportunities of the future are up for grabs.

But you have to hustle. That old mentality of "I have a college degree and a right to a job, now someone figure out how to hire and train me" won't cut it. Simply having a mentor isn't enough. To quote Andrew Carnegie, "You cannot push anyone up a ladder unless he is willing to climb." Great mentees who are willing to be their own self-advocates, navigate a world where career ladders no longer exist, and proactively tap into generational knowledge will win the opportunities of tomorrow.

It is no longer good enough to just be smart.

Having effective mentors can determine whether you start your career one step ahead, or two steps behind; on the fast-track, or running in place; in control—or just confused.

Playing catch-up is a game I know all too well.

:: MY STORY

Like most first-generation Haitian immigrants, my whole college career was spent living my parents' dream.

For those of you who are unfamiliar with Haitian households, there are only three career options: You can either become a lawyer, become a doctor, or become a nobody. But during my junior year

I realized that my parents' dreams would never make me happy or successful. Business—specifically marketing—was my passion. It was too late to switch my major, but one of my professors encouraged me to take a few business classes and become the marketing coordinator for Students in Free Enterprise, the entrepreneurship group on campus.

As a result, after graduation, I got set up with a cushy paid internship in Ohio; I even had a company car and a corporate-sponsored apartment. I was a history major who scored a marketing internship with a Fortune 500 company. Out of the 100 or so interns in the program, I was one of only three who didn't come from an Ivy League school. Game on! Life was good. For the first time, I felt like my parents were proud of me and I was finally in control of my future.

Fast-forward to my third Tuesday on the job, also known as "take the new guy to lunch" day. It was my coworker's turn, a frumpy woman named Karen.

While gleefully noodling through my Pad Thai and the obligatory, "How did you get here?" questions, I asked Karen, "Where do you see yourself in five years?"

Flashing me a look of annoyed disbelief, she shot back an icy reply: "I never hope or dream about the future because the job I want might not be there in five years."

The tone of her voice caught me off-guard. "How could someone think like that?" I wondered. "Maybe she was just upset to be having lunch with someone who was happy at work?" No one else at the office thought like that. Secretly, she became the object of my pity, so I studied her.

Karen was a loner. She had few friends in the company, and no one to show her the ropes. Corporate culture is tough for sure, but her inner beliefs and attitudes were more of a barrier to her dream job than anything else. She never connected meaningfully with anyone in the office. I promised myself that no matter what, I would never be like Karen.

Chapter One

:: JUDGMENT DAY

As the end of the summer approached, bringing my internship to an end, I was brimming with confidence. My midterm evaluations had been superb. To many in the company—and to friends, family members and especially my mom—the prospect of getting a job offer was virtually a lock.

Nothing could prepare me for what happened next.

"I'm sorry, what did you say?" I asked, perplexed, during the exit interview. The travel plans were not what I expected. There was no flight back to Ohio, just car service back to my home in Long Island.

There was no job offer. And there was no one to blame but myself. For weeks, the words of my final evaluation echoed hauntingly in my head:

➢ "Possesses extreme knowledge of the industry but lacks common sense."

➢ "Intensely gifted but rough around the edges."

➢ "Great speaker and presenter, poor decision-maker."

To everyone at the director level and above in the company, I was an asset. Based only on my presentations, reports and results, they saw a young guy who was talented, sharp, and knowledgeable.

But to those at the manager level and below, who actually worked at the office with me, I was a totally different person—an arrogant, over-achieving know-it-all with poor office etiquette.

Blowing a terrific fresh-out-of-college opportunity set me back for months. The generous salary and cushy office job were replaced with bussing tables for three dollars an hour and holding up "half-priced shoes going out of business signs" on the highway. I became depressed, and dreaded the inevitable, "Hey, what have you been doing since graduation?" question. I avoided friends, ignored emails, and wanted nothing more than to fall off the face of the earth.

Chapter One

:: **THE TURN** AROUND

One day, a good friend called me out on my pathetic moping and my refusal to take accountability for my woes.

"Bert, what happened to the big dreamer we all knew in college?" he asked.

The answer marked my breaking point: I had become what I feared most. When I looked in the mirror, I saw Karen! By acting like an embittered loner who had given up on his dream and his life, I was no different than the miserable co-worker who took me to lunch on the third Tuesday of that fateful summer.

:: **LESSONS**

That internship was my first corporate experience. It was the first time I had to buy a suit and tie for work. The expectations, office politics, and protocol were completely over my head. My professional maturity was lacking.

Worse, it was hard for me to fully commit to the position. Why? Because I never sat down to dig deep and ask myself what I really wanted to get out of it. As a result, my over-confidence in my talent blinded me to the resources all around me. The company had a great on-boarding and mentoring program; I just didn't buy into it. Looking back, it's clear that many co-workers, including my assigned mentor, Dave, had been reaching out, but I ignored their offers.

In spite of my efforts to conceal it, my weaknesses were apparent to everyone in the company—everyone except me. Dave even confided that, had I expressed more of a desire to grow and be mentored, management would have gladly worked with me to bring on board what they saw as such a talented team member. My own lack of commitment and arrogance, however, prevented me from growing.

The chief difference between me and Karen was suddenly clear. There were still people in my life refusing to let me fail, ensuring that a quick turnaround was possible. These people were my mentors; I just had to reach out to them and let them in.

With the help of several mentors, I got another shot at building my marketing experience at a direct marketing agency. I used the skills I learned there to help me build up and sell an internet startup I had founded in college. Since then, I have toured the country as a speaker, been featured in USA Today, *Young Money* magazine, and on Fox News, all before my 25th birthday.

:: WHY YOU SHOULD
LISTEN TO ME

I successfully formed over 20 mentor relationships in different areas of my life by the time I was 25. Today, I have five active mentors and two mentees. Three of my mentors are millionaires. One of my mentors was named one of *Inc. Magazine's"* 30 Entrepreneurs Under 30 this year. And another one of my mentors has been featured on Oprah.

On top of that, I have pored for hours and hours over every book, article, and tweet I could find on the topic of mentorship. The five key principles that are discussed in this book were put together by studying top young achievers in Fortune 500 companies, as well as some of *Inc.'s* Top 30 Entrepreneurs Under 30.

Imagine how much better your life, career, and mindset could be if you only knew the secrets all of these top achievers know.

Chapter One

:: WHY I WROTE THIS BOOK

What makes my message powerful is this: I never want someone to go through the feelings of worthlessness, embarrassment, and heartbreak that I suffered.

Nothing is worse than watching someone give up on their dreams because they don't see a way out. For a time, while cleaning tables for three dollars an hour, and selling watches at J.C. Penney, I couldn't see my own way out. Know this: There is always an out, and it starts with your ability to connect with the people around you who can help in order to take control of your life.

Right now, there are uniquely gifted and generous people all around you who can and will be your mentors. My fortunes didn't change until I adopted an attitude that helped me see that these people were all around me, and that they genuinely wanted to help.

Admittedly, it wasn't easy. When I first started looking into finding mentors, I was surprised at how little my friends knew about the process. For months I attended every networking event in my area and reached out to young professionals at every company I could, large and small, but I kept hearing the same things:

"How do you find a mentor, anyway? What do they do?"

"You mean the people who take you to lunch once or twice then you never hear from them again?"

I looked everywhere for a young professional's mentor manual — one that was thorough enough to make a difference but easy enough to read on a plane. No such book existed. So I decided to write it myself.

In this book I provide you with five simple principles to help you become a more marketable young professional, attract effective mentors, and consistently impress employers, business partners, and really anybody whose relationship you value in your career and your life. The next few chapters were submitted by people who used these principles to overcome obstacles and achieve success at a young age. Their stories can be yours too!

Chapter One

:: Action Step

Write down three people in your life who can take your career to the next level.

1. _____

2. _____

3. _____

What's holding you back from reaching out to them?

_____

Chapter Two:

The Unlikely Mentor

By Andrea Skerritt

I was not expecting another one of my father's routine business trips to New York to change my life. It was the summer of 2005, and I was busy preparing to spend a semester abroad, with graduation soon to follow.

I was also about to complete a summer internship at a travel public relations agency, with the understanding that my *real* goal was to enter the Music/Entertainment PR industry the following year. Deepening my contacts within the travel PR field was the furthest thought from my mind. Nevertheless, when my father asked me to join him at a media dinner coordinated by a travel PR firm to "meet some people in my field," I obliged.

That's where I met Candice Adams Kimmel, President and Founder of Adams Unlimited – a boutique public relations agency that represented a number of small Caribbean hotels and destinations, including St. Kitts – the island for which my father had recently been named Minister of Tourism. In a nutshell, my father was Candice's client. Her agency was responsible for planning and executing the event, and she was the driving force behind it all – the woman behind the steering wheel.

The way this fiery, five-foot-two-inch woman floated around Rockefeller Plaza's Sea Grill, beaming with confidence, was impressive. She effortlessly captured the attention of her dinner guests and employees, which is no small feat when my father is one of those guests, and (as I would learn years later) when you're also dealing with a group of demanding travel journalists.

A brief chat with one of Candice's employees revealed that she ruled with an iron fist, but was loved and respected by her staff. "Candice is one tough lady, but one of the smartest women you'll ever meet," I was told. Yet from where I sat, she also seemed warm, friendly and energetic. She seemed to be a Renaissance woman – a feat I had hoped to accomplish one day.

Still, there was one major force holding me back – me. My insecurities made me uncertain that I had what it would take to achieve the level of success for which I aspired. I had often been told that I was "too shy" or "too nice" to be in both the spotlight and a position of power.

"Do I have the personality it takes to run my own agency?" I wondered. I had met so many cold women in Candice's position that I had begun to believe that success in the PR industry was synonymous with being heartless, cunning and unaffected. The impression Candice left on me that night shifted my mindset, if only for a moment, and renewed my spirit. Nothing more came of that evening and I was off to study in Madrid a few weeks later. As fate would have it, however, our paths were destined to cross again.

:: **Unlikely** Reunion

Fast forward to almost two years later – the spring of 2007. Prior to this, I had somehow found myself as an Executive Trainee at a reputable healthcare PR agency in Manhattan – a far cry from the music or entertainment PR job I had hoped to secure after graduation (let's just say I wasn't prepared to work for a salary that was equivalent to a McDonald's wage). I was miserable in healthcare. No one tells you that the area of PR you decide to pursue should be one that you're passionate about even behind closed doors. If you spend every waking moment reading travel magazines, thinking about the countries you've visited and the places you've yet to explore, it would not make sense to then pursue a career in healthcare PR, would it? Travel PR would be a much better fit, no? Anyway, I digress.

Thankfully, I was able to network my way back to MMG Mardiks, the boutique travel PR agency where I had interned during the summer of 2005. Now an Account Coordinator in the field I came to realize I so loved, I thought my networking days were over, at least for the next few years. I was comfortable in my position and had the company's Vice President as my on-the-job mentor. And I could easily see myself working there for at least three to five years, so there was no need to solicit industry advice from any other source—or so I naively thought at the time.

That's why I hesitated when my father, who had been encouraging me to connect with leaders in my field, had arranged a meeting for me with the woman from the media dinner I attended with him almost two years prior. I wasn't thrilled about the forced meeting, but gave in anyway. I went to Candice's office, notebook and pen in hand, prepared for an afternoon of note-taking and uncomfortable laughter. What happened next caught me by surprise.

"Let's go somewhere for a drink," she offered. "Have you eaten?"

:: **Unlikely** Mentor

We ended up at a cozy restaurant downtown on Stone Street, where we spent hours chatting; laughing and reflecting on life, particularly my decision to reenter the world of travel PR. Several glasses of wine later, as dinner began winding down, Candice confessed that she too felt an obligation to meet with me – the client's daughter -- and had expected our meeting to be formal and uncomfortable. We laughed it off. She felt a connection to me and could sense my genuine interest in her. In return, I sensed her warm and nurturing vibe. From that evening, Candice's role in my life evolved into an interwoven mix of mentor, professional advisor and, best of all, close friend.

I have the outlook on my career and my capabilities that I have today because of my relationship with Candice Adams Kimmel. She instilled in me a confidence that I had been lacking by reassuring me about my talents and direction, from the perspective of an agency owner and industry veteran.

She also humanized for me what once seemed like an elusive and heartless role – agency President and Founder. From her I learned that it is possible to be vulnerable, passionate, and kind while still being an effective leader. Whether she's aware of it or not, she has taught me a lot about being a woman in a demanding, often grueling industry. From Candice, I learned that sometimes, the phrase "It's business, don't take it personally" doesn't always apply. It's okay to show emotion, as long as you're willing to stand up for yourself and put your foot down where it counts. And Candice taught me that seeking advice from a subordinate does not make you weak; rather, it shows strength and a willingness to learn. But most importantly, she taught me that respect, integrity and loyalty are the most important ingredients for success in this small and incestuous industry, much more so than accolades and credentials.

:: **A Closer** Look

Candice and I try to meet monthly over drinks and dinner. We maintain frequent communication, mostly via email, with the occasional "Are you alive?" phone call if one of us seems to have fallen off the face of the earth (or been swallowed by our desks). We have a relationship based primarily on friendship, but also on mutual exchange. For example, she counsels me through crucial career moves, salary and raise negotiations and leadership opportunities, while I keep her abreast of social media trends, entry-level employee concerns and the latest in Caribbean pop culture. We exchange gifts during the holidays and speak openly about our personal lives.

My relationship with Candice is a testament to the fact that every mentor relationship works differently based on the personalities of the people involved. Some people want a mentor who is all about business, who cuts to the chase and tells the industry story like it is. This approach can be intimidating, however, and I've learned it doesn't work for me. Many will end up discovering what I did – that the best and most lasting mentor relationships are with people who grow to care about you and genuinely see you as a peer and as a friend.

So what does Andrea's mentor think of Andrea? I wondered the same thing. Luckily, she was kind enough to share her thoughts.

:: **Candice on** Andrea:

There is a point in time where circumstance puts you in a position to help someone, and your life experience or situation allows you to help and affords you the privilege to share what you have. To be a mentor means that you are fortunate enough to be able to share what you have learned.

I believe all of us would like to give back – to help others –- but we are not all lucky enough to have the opportunity. When Andrea's father asked me to meet her as she was just starting her career in PR, I was provided with one of those rare opportunities in life to advise and help someone else – to share what I had learned in my career in tourism PR. Little did I expect to be learning so much myself, or that mentoring Andrea would be a two-way street, with Andrea providing me a window into the world of today's modern Caribbean woman in her early twenties: How they look at life, work, family and play, and how to balance life and work. (One area where I needed help, myself, and thus could provide no help to Andrea!)

I see a parallel between the position of female college graduates in 1970 (when I entered the workforce), when the pressure was to pursue a career as a teacher or nurse—traditional female fields—so you could always get a job, and young women today. The creative fields were not an option. Today, young Caribbean women are also encouraged to go into traditional professions where they can be successful (i.e., get a job) and creative fields are passed over.

For everything that women have accomplished in penetrating formerly male-dominated professions in the past 40 years, the pressure to pursue a traditional field where you are most likely to be successful, is still there, and doing so is more highly valued than any form of risk-taking that creative fields represent. Luckily, women like Andrea are choosing to decide for themselves and take the plunge anyway, and I'm happy to be a part of it.

Andrea is a shining light -- I always say she lights up a room. She possesses an extraordinary generosity of spirit and always has room for one more friend. She is willing to share not only herself and her time, but her family. She has made me feel like part of her extended family. Andrea is caring, nurturing, and shows an exceptional level of concern and genuine kindness towards her friends.

Chapter Two

Chapter Three:

How I Got Into MTV:
Rosangel's Story

"How did I get here?" a frustrated Rosangel Perez grumbled out loud. The former communications and production major-turned-retail manager had a nagging, terrifying concern: Had she wasted her college education? Her aspirations of working her dream job as a producer for MTV Networks seemed as unreachable as ever.

After concluding that there was no way she could use her limited experience at a retail store to get into a big company like MTV, she resigned herself to a life of night, weekend and holiday shifts. But her roommate, one of Rosangel's biggest supporters, didn't buy it. After some persuasion, she convinced Rosangel to apply for a low-level sales job at MTV. After months of persistence, Rosangel scored a temporary entry-level sales role. It still wasn't where she wanted to be, but she now really had her foot in the door. For six months, she came in early, left late, and worked her butt off. Soon enough, however, those voices crept into her head again: "Just give up, Rosie, it's too hard, you have to know someone or be somebody's daughter to get a job in production at MTV."

:: THE TURNING POINT

After sharing her story with her roommate and a few other friends, the name of a senior producer at VH1, a related company under the umbrella of Viacom, kept popping up. This producer was well-connected and known to have major input in hiring decisions. But here's the kicker: She had a reputation — a scary one. She was known for being mean, intimidating and insulting. Not the kind of woman you want to approach out of left field. As if on a loop, one thought ran through Rosangel's head for weeks: "Why would she even respond to someone like me? What could *I* do for *her?*"

One day, after yet another stressful and unfulfilling day on the job, Rosangel reached her limit. "What do I have to lose?" she thought as her nervous fingers clicked "send." She had finally emailed the producer whose name kept coming up—but she didn't ask for a job directly. Instead, this is what she said: "I have heard a lot about you and admire your leadership. Would it be okay if I took you to lunch to pick your brain sometime?"

To her amazement, the producer replied within minutes. During the meeting, Rosangel never brought up a production job; she never had to. Midway through their lunch, the producer asked for a resume and agreed to arrange an interview for Rosangel three days later.

Today, Rosangel is credited with having done production work on *MTV Cribs*.

Rosangel later learned that few people had ever approached the producer because they were scared off by her reputation. As a result, no one ever took the time to get to know her, so she was especially touched to find that Rosangel had taken a genuine interest in her career.

Stepping out of your comfort zone and introducing yourself to people is what separates those who spend their careers running in place and those who get what they want, when they want it. Rosangel's story is proof positive that mentorship is a two-way street, and both participants are richly rewarded on their journeys.

Chapter Three

Chapter Four:

How Three Mentors
Changed My Life Forever

By Ian Bel

The new economics of the 21st century put all prior beliefs to shame. The idea of long-term stability by choosing a "safe" profession – gone. The idea of loyalty from your supervisors and peers for hard work and dedication – gone. The idea that having three degrees on your wall puts you on the path to glory – gone.

But do not fret. By the very act of reading this book, it is clear that you have embraced the mindset that is required to change with it. The ideas of safety, loyalty, and longevity have not disappeared, they are only hiding. And in order to find these ideas, you must know where to look. Enter your relationships and their unrivaled ability to open doors and truly bring you success, both personally and professionally.

I was asked to write this chapter to discuss my relationships, and more specifically, my mentors. While my official professional title is "Associate at Private Equity Firm," the real value of my position is the credibility it lends me when I pursue my real job – which is to build relationships! That's the new currency for the new century.

Think about it for a second. You can't buy a job, right? WRONG. What happens when you go on an interview? How do they sort the good from the bad? They find the people you know and ask them. If you have strong relationships, then you have, in effect, bought yourself a ticket for the job. If you do not have strong relationships – well.

Thank goodness that building relationships is an acquired skill, and not determined at birth. This means that you always have the power to improve your relationships if you want to. Building relationships has everything to do with how much you care about other people and the people you surround yourself with. If you are smart, you will surround yourself with smart people and great mentors.

:: MY FIRST GREATMENTOR

If you look out your window and do not see the big tree that's full of money, then you and I grew up in the same boat. I came from a modest family, the son of two working professionals competing vigorously in the rat race, and as a result, I grew up with the mentality that a profession was the only safe career to pursue.

Unfortunately, for me, safe and boring were synonymous. Plus, I did not have a real propensity for paying attention. So I had the mentality of a natural entrepreneur. I would often pursue many opportunities at one time and reveled in the success of achieving my goals.

As a result, I learned from an early age that just because you pursue something, doesn't mean that something is worth pursuing. While I can credit myself with some great successes, I also had some momentous failures. But I did find someone who was willing to see the potential I had in my vision for my future and passion to "get things done."

My first mentor was a teacher (as all great mentors are) and a male supermodel (I bet you don't hear *that* every day!). Rashid Silvera was my eleventh grade psychology teacher who also happened to be the first African American to appear on the cover of GQ magazine back in the early 1980s. Rashid was the ultimate guru of suave – he dated supermodels, he dressed immaculately, and he was admired by all of his students. So you can imagine my intimidation: I was the exact opposite. I was awkwardly emerging from puberty, my head big and my body small. The only models I had ever seen were on a spreadsheet, and my style was questionable at best.

But as life would have it, Rashid and I had something in common: our enormous passion for creativity and the pursuit of our dreams. Rashid's dream was to be a supermodel and a teacher.

My dream was to be a filmmaker. To him, the only difference between the two of us was time.

Rashid recognized that I was shy and proactively served as my mentor. He would invite me to his office to discuss film (his best friend was Danny Glover) and talk about the various channels that I could utilize to launch myself into the film business. Eventually, I would find myself scheduling talking sessions with him regularly, in spite of my initial shyness. And I had a litany of questions prepared to talk about so we would never run out of conversation. This was the first lesson I learned about mentoring – always have questions.

Great mentors often have lifetimes' worth of experience. And many times, they have skills that they use so frequently that they do not even remember how they learned them. For that reason, it's important to squeeze out of them the experiences and skills they learned to make them what they are. Asking many different questions allows you to tease the answers out and make a quick assessment of how effective your mentor will be.

Rashid was a phenomenal mentor. He motivated me to apply to a school I never thought I would get in and taught me how to believe in myself and my potential. I realized that if I was to succeed in life, I would need many more Rashid's along the way.

:: **UNCLE** JERRY

I did not have to wait too long for my next Rashid to arrive. "Jerry" – that name probably does not mean a lot to you. But in my world, "Jerry" is as recognizable as "Madonna." Jerry is not an aging pop star though.

Rather, Jerry Nelson is an unbelievably accomplished self-made entrepreneur and philanthropist whose credits included co-founding Ticketmaster, building northern Scottsdale, Arizona and, most importantly, creating the American Leadership Academy (ALA). Every winter, while young celebrities party on the beach in Cabo San Lucas, Mexico, there is a little known place in town where young American college students receive the education of a lifetime. At the ALA, speakers are flown in from around the world to speak to a select group of students about life, business, and success. The entire week is spent interacting with these successful speakers and getting a firsthand pick of the best mentors from around the world. Naturally, I chose Jerry.

Jerry is not a young man. In fact, he is about to turn 80 years old. But you would not know this unless you were looking. He stays out until 1 a.m., drives like he just received his learner's permit and travels the country speaking to thousands of college students – FOR FREE. But my first experience with Jerry was not of random chance. I had to work for it.

This is the second thing I learned about great mentors. You have to work for them. Not literally work for them, but you have to work to earn their respect and the relationship itself.

I first learned about Jerry as a freshman in college. I heard the stories of students who were star-struck by the amazing wealth that Jerry had achieved – and his even greater willingness to give it away. Jerry loved to teach people how to win and succeed in life. All he required were willing participants, and there were many. So when I had my first chance to meet him at a fraternity conference in Iowa, I jumped on it.

As it turned out, my friend Ian was moderately close to Jerry and I pushed him hard to introduce me. I think at first Ian was a bit hesitant. I don't think he wanted the competition for Jerry's already short attention span. But he introduced me anyway.

The first morning of the conference, I walked into a grand lobby and in the center of the floor was a gray-haired man surrounded by roughly 30 college students. I knew it was him! My heart was racing; I couldn't believe it. Here was a man who had more money than I could dream of, and he was only 50 feet away! I slowly moved towards him, my heart ready to jump out of my shirt. I nudged Ian and said, "Do it, do it!"

Ian smiled and gently tugged Jerry's arm. "Hey! How are you?" Jerry asked, clearly not remembering Ian's name. Ian replied, "I am well, but there is someone I would like to introduce you to." Jerry turned to me and with a quirky teenage smile said, "When are you coming to Cabo?!" I couldn't believe it! Cabo? Mexico? At 19? Immediately, without hesitation and with little thought I said, "When would you like me to?"

That was the first lesson I learned from Jerry. Act on the moment. Jerry rewarded my initiative with: "See you in January!" And then he walked away.

:: A VERY RICH MAN WHO HAPPENED TO HAVE A LOT OF MONEY

Jerry ended up teaching me a lot about life. He taught me that you only get as much as you ask for. He taught me that you can be a garbage man if you wish, and it is a very respectable job – BUT YOU DON'T NEED TO GO TO COLLEGE TO BE A GARBAGE MAN.

Chapter Four

Jerry taught me not to squander time, since it's the most important resource we have. Jerry taught me to always finish my food because somewhere people are starving, and they would love to be holding my plate. Jerry taught me urgency and action and that the line between success and failure is often determined by who shows up and who doesn't.

Most importantly, though, Jerry taught me that wealth and success has little to do with the size of your bank account. It has everything to do with your ability to set high goals – and to achieve them.

Jerry loved to give his money away. In fact, he felt more pleasure in giving his money away than he ever felt earning it. Growing up, I had often heard the question, "Who do you want to be when you are older?" To me, this was a silly question. I did not want to be anyone other than me. But I did find that there were *qualities* of people that I wanted, or a certain talent for accomplishment that I wanted to have in my own toolbox.

In selecting a great mentor, it is important to identify which of these skills and talents you want to have—and to find the people who have them. It's very unlikely that you'll find all of the skills and talents you are looking for in one mentor (if you do, please let me know who that is). You must constantly be on the search for these types of people. This will only make the search easier, however, because you will naturally know what types of questions to ask. *How did you gain that skill? How did you figure out how to handle that situation?*

The qualities I saw in Jerry were ones I wanted to have. I wanted to feel the passion for life that he did. I wanted to get up at 5 a.m. and love every waking moment. Jerry taught me all of these things and that everyone – EVERYONE – was capable of achieving them. There is no such thing as have and have-nots, only can and cannots.

Every time I spoke to Jerry I felt energy, a rush of confidence that propelled me to succeed. The feeling was intense and enormous and, ultimately, stayed with me long after I continued to see him. To Jerry, helping people succeed was the greatest privilege in the world. And to him, having that ability made him a very rich man. He did not care about material possessions, only about those that were around him.

Chapter Four

This mindset allowed Jerry to feel unconditional love for his life and allowed him to be truly rich. So, as it turned out, Jerry had been rich his whole life. The only difference was at the end when he actually had money – even if only for a short time.

:: IF IT IS TO BE, IT IS UP TO ME

I have learned that there are circles of great mentors you have in your life. Some will guide you through specific professional paths; others will be there when you need them emotionally. Some you speak with daily and others you speak to once a year. It's important to have all kinds of great mentors in your life, and having many mentors does not mean that one or the other is more effective.

I have been blessed to have many different mentors in my life— and now, many mentees as well. While Jerry was a fantastic mentor on a large scale, I needed someone closer to home for more personal issues.

Ironically, Jerry's best friend, Paul Wineman, fit the bill. Paul was no stranger to success. He served in the military as a Green Beret, he is a world-renowned professional contract negotiator, and he survived not one but TWO plane crashes. Paul was not the socialite that Jerry was, however. And while I had to work hard for Jerry's relationship, I had to work even harder for Paul's. I didn't even had the chance to meet him until my junior year of college.

Paul was a celebrity in my world. I had read his book on negotiation and even put his theory to work – albeit not very well at first. So the night I saw Paul sitting at a bar, I grabbed a bottle of beer and headed over to his table. There was nothing overly impressive about him. He was wearing a white collared shirt and khaki shorts – seemingly immersed in the peace of the moment. Naturally, I could not wait for him to emerge from his trance, so I borrowed a move from my friend Ian and nudged his arm.

He turned to me and smiled. With a deep-barreled voice he said, "Well hello there, how are you doing tonight?" I thought I had just entered a cheesy PBS show. I said, "I am doing great! And I wanted to meet you so I came up to you to introduce myself." He smiled some more and said, "Well then, please, introduce."

Chapter Four

That's how my relationship with Paul Wineman was born. There was no magic trick, no gimmicks. As with all relationships, it only required a little initiative. Paul and I spent a lot of time in the years after our meeting talking specifics about how to handle conflict situations. I would ask him very specific questions about a situation. Such as, "How did you know he was going to come down in price and not walk away from you?" Paul would answer, "I had no idea if he would walk away or not, but I did know I had five other options waiting for me in case I did!"

Paul felt free enough to tell me anything. And this is exactly the type of relationship that I think great mentors have with their mentees. You must work hard to earn your mentor's trust, and you should not treat them any differently than you would a friend or colleague. The best mentor relationships I have had required a high level of comfort where there was no fear of judgment or opinion -- only the shared passion to mutually improve each other's lives.

This is the final lesson that I will share with you: Great mentors are not a one-way ticket. For as much insight and knowledge as you will gain from them, they will be equally fulfilled to have the chance to share it.

Most people in this world are too afraid or too self-absorbed to go out of their way to ask people their advice or ask them to be their mentor. For those who go the distance, they will find that a great life lies ahead of them. Rashid, Jerry and Paul are all credited self-less mentors for their success in life, and in turn, I credit them for the success I have had in my life.

Being a member of the cycle of mentoring is a privilege that most do not get to experience. If you are lucky enough to take the advice and experience taught in this book and apply it to your life, I have no doubt that you will achieve far greater things than you ever thought were possible.

If there is one lesson that I can leave you with that I think embodies the cans from the can-nots, the winners from the losers, and the great from the good, it is a person's ability to have confidence in themselves and to take initiative on their own. As Paul has taught me countless times, ultimately, there is only one person who will determine whether or not you succeed in life – and that person is you. *If it is to be, it is up to me.*

Chapter Four

:: LESSONS
LEARN ANYTHING?

Although Andrea, Rosangel, and Ian had different stories, all of them embraced mentors with a positive attitude, took initiative in the relationship, and looked for ways to give value to their mentors.

Do that and no one can stop you. You will find throughout this book that I refer back to these stories and the principles these young achievers used to live their dreams.

Each story reflected the life-changing lessons we can learn from mentors. Ian learned to follow his passion and act on the moment. Rashid encouraged him to apply for a school he would have never normally applied to, and Jerry gave him the confidence to agree to a trip to Cabo before he had any idea how he would pay for it or get there.

Andrea learned that she could be tough and caring, an authority and a woman all at the same time. Her story also taught us that you can have as much of an impact on your mentor as they have on you. Most importantly, she learned she could follow her dream in Travel PR.

Rosangel's sincerity shined and scored her a dream job. By overcoming her fears and making a genuine effort to get to know an executive that many people thought was scary and unapproachable, she took her career to new plateaus and made a friend along the way.

All of these stories can be your story. If you embrace mentors with a positive attitude, that day will come sooner than you think.

Chapter Five:

The Number One Belief
That All Successful People
Share *(Beeattitudes)*

We human beings are social beings.
We come into the world
as a result of other's actions...
Whether we like it or not,
there is hardly a moment
of our lives when we do not benefit
from others activities.
For this reason,
it is hardly surprising that most of our
happiness arises in the context
of our relationships with others."

Dalai Lama

:: IT STARTS WITH ATTITUDE

Our first order of business is to discuss your attitudes toward people already in your life who could potentially become mentors. How do you view them? Are they merely pawns on a chess board, waiting to be used at your whim, or are they like bees, strategically bonding together, and contributing to the larger success of the beehive?

You are going to hear me talk a lot about "attitude" in this book. That's because I believe that having the right attitude and set of inner beliefs is crucial to attracting successful mentors. Every CEO, millionaire, and mogul believes that internal success is the foundation of external success—and it starts with your attitude.

:: THE PARABLE OF THE BEES

Honeybees are the most productive community in all of nature. These little farmers pollinate over half of the foods we eat. If you gave them suits, office space, and paid them a minimum wage salary, they would represent a one trillion dollar industry!

It's no secret that many of the answers to life's questions can be found in nature.

Dating as far back as the time of Egyptian Pharoahs, up to current research at Cornell University, humans have always looked to honeybees for the secret to success. Honeybees are also the official celebrity on the box of Honey Nut Cheerios, which I think is pretty awesome!

What lessons can we learn from tiny fuzzy creatures with brains the size of a spec?

In the beehive, honeybees practice three success principles I like to call the Beeatitudes.

Chapter Five

BEEATTITUDES

1. **Share Knowledge, Skills, and Know-how-**

   To survive the hive you have to share. Honeybees pass along information about changes in temperature and the location of water. Since they live only a few weeks long, they have to quickly transfer "know-how" to other bees or the whole hive falls apart. Every successful company works the same way. As older generations of employees get ready to leave, they transfer knowledge and skills to a new class of hungry go-getters. That's you, right?

2. **Collaborate-**

   On its own, a single bee is useless for honey production and pollinating flowers. That takes collective effort of the entire hive to do that. No hierarchy here, just a flat system where each bees does its part to support the others and produce sweet results. If you ask anyone who works at Zappos or 37 Signals, they will describe the company culture in the exact same way.

3. **Enlightened Self-Interest-**

   Honeybees share a belief that every successful CEO, millionaire, and top achiever shares: that we have a mutual stake in each others success. When a bee finds food, it doesn't just feed itself and keep it moving. Honeybees can do a special dance in complete darkness to communicate the exact distance, direction, and location of food to all the others in the hive.

   Candace Savage, a Nobel Prize-winning scientist who authored the book BEES calls this phenomenon enlightened self-interest. That's the secret sauce. The magic will happen in your life when you start to view people, not as stepping stones for your personal agenda, but as mutual partners in your success,

If they win, you win.

Picture for a moment what it looks like inside the bee-hive. Some 70,000 bees counting on each other's efforts to survive. Some bees exclusively forage for food, others fan air into the hive or scout for places to build new hives. Worker bees babysit the larvae while Queen bees manage the operation. Enlightened self-interest holds the hive together.

Enlightened self-interest makes the hive the most productive community in all of nature-a community we could all learn from.

WHAT THIS MEANS FOR YOU

Want to turbo charge your productivity? Think about how the Beeattitudes could apply to you. What if you had someone like Rosangel's mentor at VH1, who always shared information about job opportunities in your industry?

Or imagine you could string together a top hive like Ian did in chapter 4. You'll recall that his mentors, Rashid, Jerry and Paul, frequently collaborated with him, gave him feedback, and helped him to pick up skills like improved confidence and negotiating strategies--attributes which benefited him at the Private Equity Firm.

Do you see why your attitude towards mentors is so important? Imagine for one moment if Andrea followed her initial idea to go it alone and not meet with Candice. She probably would have been stuck in a job that didn't fully engage her brilliance. She certainly would have missed out on a friend.

All three were more productive, satisfied and happy in their lives because they followed the principles of the hive.

It takes guts to reach out for help. It takes guts to work with others, and even more courage to admit that you don't know it all. If you view success as an individual achievement, you may thrive, but you will almost certainly miss out on a special opportunity to tap into your inner greatness.

Chapter Five

Next time you see a dysfunctional company or group of people, hang out and observe their attitudes. Are they like honeybees? And more importantly, do they follow the principles of the hive?

Yes, this is a book about success and finding mentors; but before you can look outside to build relationships, you must look within. It is only when we genuinely adopt the attitude that we have a stake in each other's success (enlightened self-interest) and we practice the principles of the hive that we make ourselves magnetic to those around us—those who can unlock our inner greatness. Who's in your top hive?

this could be you :)

Honey Bee

Chapter Five

Chapter Six:

Why Should I Care
About Finding Mentors?

:: HOW TO WIN
IN THE NEW ECONOMY

If you take a close look, our world today keeps developing more and more similarities to the hive. Information moves at warp speed. Our livelihoods now depend on information transfer. The traits that guaranteed us success in the past – hard work, dedication, intelligence – are no longer enough. The ability to share information, skills and know-how, collaborate, and build mutually supportive hives that hold each other accountable is the new game in town.

So how did we get here?

In Daniel Pink's groundbreaking book *A Whole New Mind: Why Right Brainers Will Rule the Future*, he explains:

There has been a shift in the skills that society values. The analytical left-brain thinking, or "hard skills" valued in the 1970s will no longer be enough to get ahead. Given the reality of where the world is going, "softer skills" like empathy and collaboration are now in demand. White-collar jobs are being outsourced to and automated by emerging countries and computers respectively.

Essentially, not only do we have to find more ways to differentiate ourselves, but we have to master skills that computers can't do better, faster or cheaper. According to Forrester Research, at least 3.3 million white-collar jobs and $136 billion dollars in wages will shift from the U.S. to low-cost countries such as India, China and Russia by 2015. Yikes!

What does this all mean to you? It means that if we keep on doing what we've been doing, we risk being replaced.

Companies are finally starting to figure out that these so-called "soft skills" impact the bottom line. A recent survey of major Fortune 500 companies from Apple to Unilever revealed that top companies are looking for specific 21st century skills in their new hires, but these "survival skills" are NOT taught in schools. IBM has made knowledge transfer and mentorship one of their top global initiatives. They actively seek to hire people who are not only intelligent but who are also able to value and work with mentors.

Chapter Six

:: WHY IS FINDING YOUR OWN MENTORS IMPORTANT?

The world looks different than it did a generation ago. Your parents don't recognize the world we live in. Neither do most of your managers.

We are the migration generation, and this generational shift in expectations has indelibly changed the relationship between young professionals and the companies they work for. In his book *Tribes*, Seth Godin sums up the last 10 years neatly:

Many people are starting to realize that they work a lot and that working on stuff they believe in (and making things happen) is much more satisfying than just getting a paycheck and waiting to get fired (or die).

Gone are the days where people stayed at one company for 20 years and received a gold Rolex for their loyalty. Gone are the days where one manager had the time to mold you and help you develop and tap into your potential. Today, the average twenty-something changes jobs three to four times before hitting 30.

The problem is, the average manager not only knows this, but is annoyed by it. She is skeptical of you, overworked, stressed out, and too bogged down with the unrealistic demands of her job to invest much time in developing someone who won't even stick around.

This radically different, faster-paced employee landscape has changed the mentor/mentee relationship too—but mostly for the better. Mentoring is now less intimidating. It must now be collaborative and highly reciprocal, based on knowledge sharing and mutual support—making it a more attractive and worthwhile relationship for both people.

Today's top achievers and top companies already get it. Take, for example, McKinsey & Company. They have stayed ahead of the mentoring curve with a program where they encourage new employees to assemble a team of five or six peers, managers, and mentors who are close in age and dedicated to the success of each member of the group.

Chapter Six

In a sense, these young professionals are building a hive. The enlightened self-interest and collaboration fostered by their arrangements is priceless. The challenge for you is to establish the same collaborative environment on your own.

Where do you find your mentors? The first step is to define what a mentor really does. But before we do that, let's first look at what's at risk if we ignore the benefits of building beehives.

:: THE COST OF NOT
HAVING MENTORS

There are two types of people in the workplace – those with low-skill growth and those with high-skill growth. Whichever one you choose to be, you should know what it means for your pocket. The average person's salary in the United States increases 3 percent a year. Why only 3 percent?

According to *Million Dollar Habits* by Brian Tracy, most people develop just enough skills to survive their first year on the job and not get fired. They never grow past that; instead, they only repeat tasks at the same skill level for the next 25 years. Doesn't it make sense then that the salary of a low-skill growth person only rises as fast as inflation? The good news is that you're still able to double your income this way. The bad news is that it would take you 25 years to do it!

High-skill growth people, on the other hand, average a 15 to 25 percent salary increase per year. They double their income too, only much more quickly.

Mentors and successful relationships are critical to skill growth. Studies show that good mentors help you to develop skills faster, learn tasks more quickly, build key relationships, and become more productive in your career. Becoming a high-skill growth person involves understanding how to find and learn from good mentors and taking ownership of your development. In the new economy, career ladders don't exist. You have to build your own.

Chapter Six

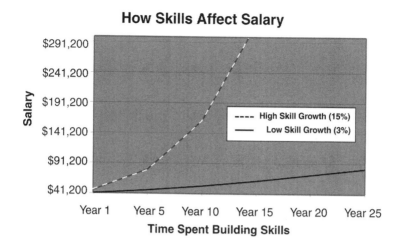

How Skills Affect Salary

:: **SO WHAT IS A MENTOR**
ANYWAY?

Over the years, the word mentorship has become associated with intimidation. How did this happen? It seems that our cultural views have created a superiority complex revolving around mentorship, which in turn makes mentors seem unapproachable.

There are many reasons why we avoid mentors. You might worry about disappointing people. You might feel small in the face of someone so successful, or too embarrassed to ask others for help. But I believe the main problem has to do with the word's definition.

As an experiment, I visited a local high school and Starbucks near a college to discover the average person's reaction to the word "mentor."

Some of the more interesting responses were:

➢ "Guidance counselor"

➢ "Know-it-all"

➢ "Someone better/smarter than me"

➢ "Mr. Feeney"

Chapter Six

Reread that last bullet. (Go on... I'll wait.)

Mr. Feeney!! Remember that guy? He was the grumpy teacher from the American TV show "Boy Meets World." The one who rocked stuffy corduroy jackets like they were going out of style. He always knew what was best for his students—or so he thought.

For most people, a "mentor" is a person exactly like Mr. Feeney: a teacher or authority figure with more experience and power. That wouldn't be such a bad definition if American culture didn't distort the student/teacher relationship. Think back to elementary school. Do you remember how the teacher was always right and you were always wrong? We are trained to mindlessly repeat the lessons of authority figures in school, and it leaves a bad taste in our mouths.

The only way to understand mentorship is to look above and beyond our experiences with teachers and the education system. A true mentor isn't some egotistical know-it-all "teacher" in a plaid jacket trying to impose his beliefs on you. A true mentor is someone who draws out the genius *already* inside of you. A mentor gives you the emotional confidence to tap into your own inner greatness.

It is crucial to realize that all of the growth, discovery, and success from the mentor relationship will come from within you, not your mentor. All the good stuff is already there, just waiting to be discovered.

Self-discovery has always been the cornerstone of true education and teaching, and a healthy mentor relationship is based on you taking ownership of your ideas. In turn, the mentor should be respectful of your experience. Ultimately, this collaboration results in your ability to set out on your own path, albeit with their support and guidance. Rather than being a passive student, you become an active collaborator, engaged in drawing out your inner genius.

The Peter Thomas book Be Great hammers this point home. He quotes Glenn Clark's *The Man Who Tapped the Secrets of the Universe:*

I believe sincerely that every man [and woman] has a consummate ge-

nius within him [or her]. Some appear to have it more than others only because they are aware of it more than others are, and the awareness or unawareness of it is what makes each one of them masters or holds them down to mediocrity.*

* I changed this quote to include "and women" and "or her" because the majority of old school quotes exclude women. Not cool.

Leadership coach John C. Maxwell likes to say that mentors draw the best out of you—literally. They:

> ➢ B elieve in you

> ➢ E ncourage you

> ➢ S upport you

> ➢ T ell you the truth even when it hurts

Mentors can help you with:

> ➢ Discovering your true strengths

> ➢ Finding the right job or opportunities

> ➢ Making key introductions

> ➢ Exposing you to new life-changing experiences

> ➢ Identifying the skills you need to reach your goals

> ➢ Acting as a sounding board to vent or bounce ideas

> ➢ Drawing out your inner genius

> ➢ Encouragement and accountability

:: HERE IS WHAT
WE KNOW:

According to studies on mentoring outcomes, mentees in well-matched mentorships report achieving more social and career opportunities.

Chapter Six

-Sun Microsystems concluded a study of 1,000 employees over a five-year period that found that **mentees are five times more likely to be promoted** than new hires that don't have mentors.

-The same study found that **employees with mentors are 20 percent more likely to get a raise** than those without one.

-Catalyst Research found that men and women who had mentors were more likely to start their first post-MBA job in higher positions than those without a mentor.

In other words, mentoring works! And it works especially well when it's done right. In later chapters, we will discuss how to find the best type of mentor for you, and what qualities they must possess to ensure success.

Chapter Six

Chapter Seven:

Don't Let Your Friends Sting You!

:: FRIENDS MATTER

Most people want to see you succeed because they view your success as part of their success. In other words, they share the Beeattitudes of honeybees. So why does everyone you run into seem like such a drag?

The answer starts with you. Who do you allow yourself to be around? If you hang out with negative, cynical people, you probably think everybody is out to get you.

Am I saying there are no cutthroat people out there? Of course not. But there are far fewer of them than you think.

:: WHAT DOES THIS ALL MEAN?

Your friends, especially the ones you keep in your twenties, exert considerable influence over you and over how you perceive others. Motivational speaker Brian Tracy calls these people your reference group. Typically when you want advice, have a new idea, or start dating someone new, you consult your reference group first.

A negative reference group can be fatal. If every time your mentor puts a good idea in your left ear, your friends drizzle poison in your right, what do you think will happen? Every one step forward will come with two steps back.

:: BEE LIKE WATER

Bruce Lee, the world's most famous martial artist, said, "Be formless... shapeless, like water. If you put water into a cup, it becomes the cup. You put water into a bottle; it becomes the bottle. You put it into a teapot; it becomes the teapot. Water can flow, and it can crash."

Your friends and relationships help determine the shape you take. You are the water.

If you put yourself in a group of super achievers, you will be a super achiever. If you put yourself in a group of underachievers, you will be an underachiever. For this reason, it's important to keep all of your relationships in perspective before you start to build a bee-hive. Before you can build meaningful mentor relationships, you must give some thought to who you spend your time with and how it affects you. If you aren't choosing friends who support instead of sabotage you, you will probably choose the wrong mentors too.

Am I saying to get rid of your friends? No, but I am saying you need to be mindful about who you spend the majority of your time with. If you're honest with yourself, you will recognize that certain people do actually weigh you down and drain your energy. To stay on track, you may have to learn to love a few people from a distance.

:: Action Step
See The True Impact
of Your Friends.

The Rule of 5

Tony Robbins likes to say that you are the average of the five people with whom you spend the most time. Think about that. Make a list of the five people you spend the most time with.

Name of Person #1 _____

Name of Person #2 _____

Name of Person #3 _____

Name of Person #4 _____

Name of Person #5 _____

I want you to draw an arrow next to each person-facing up if they inspire you and make you a better person, facing down if they bring you down. What did you learn?

Chapter Seven

Now that we understand the foundations of the attitudes and support systems we need to build mentor relationships, let's debunk a few myths about what it means to have a mentor.

You must learn from the mistakes of others. You can't possibly live long enough to make them all yourself.
-Sam Levenson

Chapter Eight:

Outdated But Still True Myths
About Mentors

Rudy is a recruiter at a major rental car company. One morning, he walks into a conference room and asks his newly hired staff, "Who could use a mentor?" Pride silences the room. Not one hand rises. Switching his strategy, employing just a slight hint of exasperation, he poses the following questions:

"How many of you like having someone to vent to after a rough day?"

Reluctantly, a few hands go up.

"How many of you would appreciate having someone in the company who recognizes your efforts, shares it with management and helps you get promoted quicker?"

A couple more hands squeak up.

"How many people like having other people they can collaborate with to solve mutual challenges?" That one really gets their attention. About half the people in the room raise their hands.

Why the change of heart? The first question Rudy asked led them to think, "What's all this mentor talk? Aren't I good enough?"

All Rudy did differently the second time around was to sidestep using the word "mentor" by focusing on the practical benefits of having one. And it made a world of difference.

Most of us actually want the benefits of a mentor, but no one actually wants a "mentor." The word brings up those familiar feelings of insecurity that are so ingrained in us.

:: THE "I" GENERATION

We Millennials wildly overestimate our ability to succeed on our own. Michael Jordan had a shooting coach, Muhammad Ali had a trainer, and Will Smith had an acting mentor. Where does the overconfidence of our generation come from?

Modern success stories have been neatly packaged to fit a "me first" mentality that then gets shoved down our throats.

Evelyn McDonnell, a former writer for *The Village Voice*, attributes our confidence to the cockiness of youth. We have a newfound infatuation with the Horatio Alger do-it-yourself story. We think this is uniquely American and uniquely cool.

Think about where society is going. How do we listen to music? On an Ipod.

What do we use to make calls? On an Iphone.

Where will you see the new "Dark Knight" movie in 3D? At the Imax.

Society has always seduced us with the myth of the self-made person, but with the emergence of personal technology and "me first" brand messages, it has become increasingly difficult to separate myth from reality.

Of course you don't want help from others. Of course you feel inadequate when you reach out to others. Why wouldn't you? Eminem became a platinum rapper by himself. Octomom parades her plan to raise eight kids on her own. Barack Obama picked himself up by his bootstraps and became president.

Or so we're told. The image of a self made-man (or woman) is the core of Mafia legacy and pop culture. We think it's cool. And it is cool. It's just not *true*.

People think of Mark Zuckerberg, the founder of Facebook, as a lone Harvard hero who connected the world from his dorm room. What people don't realize is that Mark had the guidance of two internet giants, Peter Thiel (founder of Paypal) and Sean Parker (co-founder of Napster) during the critical beginning stages of Facebook.

Three big myths surrounding the word mentor distort our view of success.

:: Myth 1
Mentors Are For Losers

While few will admit it, many people secretly believe that if they're told they need a mentor, it's because someone thinks they're a loser. This myth is reinforced by images in popular culture. I recently rewatched "Dangerous Minds" with Michelle Pfeiffer.

It's your standard clichéd Hollywood movie: An idealistic inner-city teacher sticks her neck out to mentor a class of student rejects, hoping to change their lives. The lingering image from the movie is that of a teacher, played by Michelle Pfeiffer, giving special treatment to these kids—because something is wrong with them. They "need" help.

No parents, drug habits, immigration issues, gang violence—these are just some of the challenges the characters face. Most of the funding out there for mentoring programs targets underperforming students, which means you often see real classrooms that resemble the one in "Dangerous Minds."

If you were in one of those classrooms, you would probably think, "Why am I here with all the screw-ups? Is something wrong with me too?"

Believe me, I know the feeling. Growing up, I was in an English as a Second Language. class. They assigned us a special mentor and put all of us in a similarly bright little room in the corner of the school. How could you not feel like a loser, singled out for your inadequacy?

What is the end result of being spoon-fed these images in popular culture? The obvious conclusion is that if you're assigned a "helper" or mentor, then it's because you suck at life. We grow up with these silent, dangerous beliefs. Is it any wonder why we hesitate to find these people on our own?

As we discussed earlier in the book, however, this attitude simply won't cut it in today's competitive environment. So what can we do today to change this mindset? We can start by asking better questions.

:: AM I REALLY
NOT GOOD ENOUGH?

The reason it's so easy for us to buy into the myth that mentors are for losers is that it plays to our basic psychology. The two most powerful human motivators are survival and security. Whenever we hear the word mentor, just like the word "tutor," we feel threatened. In this culture, asking for help is a sign of weakness—so when someone offers it, we get defensive. As a result, our knee-jerk reaction is to ask, "Aren't I good enough to do it on my own?" The truth is it takes more guts and courage to ask for help than to shun it. "Aren't I good enough?" is also a passive question, one with limited use.

The better question to ask is, "Can I be better?" It's an active question which pushes and challenges us. Mark Zuckerberg, Bill Gates and LeBron James have all pursued mentors and advisors, precisely because they answered "yes" to that last question.

:: THE TRUTH

In conclusion, the myth that mentors are for losers simply misses the mark. Mentors benefit anyone who answers yes to the question, "Can I be better?" Every successful CEO and noteworthy person in history has benefited from mentors of one kind or another. There is no shame in succeeding with the help of others.

:: Myth 2:
Mentors Are Saviors

You just found your million-dollar mentor. Hooray! Now what? If you're like some of the people I interviewed, you probably think you're all set. Unfortunately, many people aren't interested in building relationships anymore, just in getting ahead. We have fallen into the mindset that all we need to do is find the right "stepping stone" or person to help us climb the ladder of success, and the job is done.

Once we've found this person, we can just kick back our sandy flip-flops and begin sipping frozen drinks through multi-colored umbrella straws. But there are no shortcuts in life. Here are some practical reasons why this attitude is a dead end:

> ➢ The idea that you can find one person who is your mentor, pastor, accountant, and love guru, all in one, is both unrealistic and a surefire recipe for disappointment. It's also pretty annoying. Many mentors I interviewed for this book (who happen to be people, just like you) felt strongly about this.

Mike Robinson, founder of ProximityMatch.com, and sought-after mentor, put it bluntly:

"The biggest mistake people make is thinking that a mentor can solve all their problems...I'll gladly help but know what you're coming to me for and be ready to work. If you're coming to me for relationship advice, don't expect me to do your taxes. Anyone would be annoyed by that."

➤ The concept of mentors as "saviors" gives us a warped idea of success. It overlooks the roles hard work and personal responsibility play in the mentor-mentee relationship. The employee who has the best career network still has to show up early and produce. The student with the best academic support still studies. The Casanova with the best love guru still has to send flowers on Valentine's Day. Let me spell it out for you: YOU STILL HAVE TO DO STUFF.

:: Myth 3:
But I Have Nothing To Offer Anyone

Most people just aren't very good at assessing their own value. In fact, we're typically smarter and more capable than we give ourselves credit for. Research by Ferrazzi Greenlight, a think tank on relationships, shows that humans tend to underestimate our knowledge in certain areas.

So how do you tackle this myth that you have nothing to offer? You do it by discovering your strengths, becoming a resource, and *giving* value before you get value. We will talk about how to do that in detail in later chapters. All of these steps are covered in my five pillars for finding mentors.

Mastering these principles will make you a steal for any employer. In the next five chapters, you will discover the secrets to achieving results in your life faster than ever before. I call this system STING.

STORY-How to discover and tell your story in a way that wins friends, admirers, and allies.

TYPE- What types of people you should or shouldn't approach for mentoring.

Chapter Eight

INTRODUCTION-How to introduce yourself like a champion to EVERYONE you meet EVERY time (including done-for-you scripts you can use for instant results!).

NURTURE-Tips for nurturing mentor relationships that deliver opportunities and timely connections.

GRATITUDE-How gratitude can dramatically improve your happiness and your relationships.

What are you waiting for? Turn the page and let's get started!

 After presenting at a high energy half-day seminar for the National Chamber Foundation a gentleman named T.J. came up to me and asked an interesting question.

Q : Am I using People When I ask for help?

A : That attitude misses the mark.

We tend to think that reaching out to someone makes us look like a "user." Here is a different way to look at asking for help.

Professional speaker Tony Robbins likes to share a story about an unusual dinner guest. The man had attended one of his workshops and Tony was well aware that he was considerably wealthier than him. As a nice gesture he offered to pay for dinner. The modestly dressed man refused. When Tony insisted he got a wake up call. "Don't you DARE take away my privilege to pay for your meal!" the man growled.

The lesson here is that it is selfish to deny someone the privilege to GIVE. Giving makes us feel good. One of the best gifts you can give is allowing someone to give to you. How many people in your life right now would help you out if you only let them?

Chapter Eight

No matter what you do in your life, what you create, what career you have, whether you have a family or kids, or make a lot of money...your greatest creation is always going to be your life's story."

–Jonathan Harris, artist

Chapter Nine:

How To Discover And Tell Your Story

In A Way That Wins Friends, Admirers, And Allies.

I never thought that 17 words could change my relationship with my own mentor forever.

"So what do you want to do with your life?" my mentor asked. It was during one of our first conversations, and I gave what I thought was a smart and well-researched answer.

"Now what do you *really* want to do?" he insisted.

Clearly, he saw right through my answer. He wanted me to stop trying to impress him. This guy was one of the senior people at a huge brand-name company. What could I even have to impress him with, anyway?

Annoyed and nervous, I blurted out, "Help people. I just, I just want to help people. If I'm sure about anything, it's that."

Those words changed our relationship forever. After he heard my second answer, he genuinely wanted to help me—because he knew my *real* story.

Who are you really? What do you want? What is your story? You should be able to answer these questions honestly if you want to take your career to the next level. Can you?

For most people, these are "I'll-get-to-it-when-I-get-the-chance-to" type of questions. But by focusing on these questions today, you can create results that are almost magical. People don't care about how smart you are, or how detailed your career path is. But they *will* care about your story. After all, everybody likes a good story.

Take the clothing brand TOMS Shoes. People don't buy the shoes because of how they look – no offense, but they look pretty plain— they buy them because they like the founder Tom's story. With every pair of shoes you purchase, he donates one pair of shoes to a child in need in an underdeveloped country. Simple, direct and persuasive, it makes a great brand story.

Another Tom, Tom Szaky — the founder of Terracycle — rose to fame by selling fertilizer. I don't know about you, but that doesn't sound particularly exciting to me. The real fleshed-out story, however, is pretty cool. He was a broke college student who sold warm poop inside used soda bottles to help realize his vision of saving and sustaining our planet.

Chapter Nine

When you hear that version, he instantly transforms into someone you'd be interested in talking to. Stories are people-magnets, and there is no reason you shouldn't take advantage of their power.

The rest of this chapter will focus on how to create a "magnetic story" that will have people literally fighting over themselves to mentor you. If you have a compelling story and vision and you share it, you will naturally attract those people who share your core values, the same people who can help skyrocket your career. Doing some homework and approaching the right people will make it much more likely that you hit it off with your future mentors.

:: STEP 1

FORGET EVERYTHING YOU WERE TAUGHT IN GRADE SCHOOL, FIGURE OUT YOUR "WHO"

Most of us can remember a point in our childhood when someone asked us that classic question "What do you want to be when you grow up?" In fifth grade, I wanted to be an astronaut. You probably also thought about what you wanted to be at an early age.

Big mistake. This question takes us away from both what we really want and what makes us truly happy. When we are trained to focus so much on *what* we want to be, we forget to focus on *who* we want to be.

You will impress far more people by knowing your values, goals, and beliefs about the person you want to become than you will by your ability to rattle off your achievements. This is the most important part of your "story," and unfortunately we've been taught to think about this in the wrong way.

So how do you figure out *who* you want to be? Stop focusing on what you want to do or have, and start focusing on how you feel about the person you actually are.

Here's why: When we focus on the cars, jewelry, houses and dream jobs, we overlook the fact that none of those things are what really makes us happy. Look around you; I'm sure you can find someone who has your dream job, car, or spouse, and is absolutely miserable. By the same token, you can also find someone with much less materially and financially than you, who is as happy as a dog with a steak sandwich.

Do you remember when Michael Jackson died? It seemed like every day, there was a new special called "The Tragic Life of Michael Jackson" or some variation on that theme. Did you ever ask yourself how the wealthiest musician of our time — the guy owned his own theme park! — could live such a tragic and lonely life? Now I've been following Michael since he was black, and I can't recall a single time when he was happy. I believe the real tragedy was that he never felt at peace with who he was.

It's not the car we want, the theme park, or even the corner office; it's the "feeling" that these things bring us. Those feelings are what we crave. Being the person you want to be gives you those "feelings" of success, and that will matter more in the end than any possession or job title.

And the best part is, when you feel this way about yourself, others feel it too, and they are automatically drawn to you. That's the secret sauce! People enjoy helping authentic people who know *who* they are and what they really want in life.

What are three things you want people to remember about you on your deathbed?

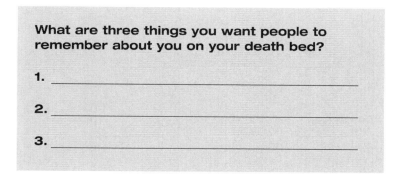

What are three things you want people to remember about you on your death bed?

1. _____

2. _____

3. _____

Chapter Nine

:: IT WORKS!

I first learned about the exercise described above at a high-energy event put on by the Extreme Entrepreneurship Tour. Something incredible happened: A man named Casey stood up — he hadn't said one word during the entire conference — and started shedding tears as he read his tombstone out loud.

"Here lies a man who provided a better life for his children than he had." Casey, whom people used to call "white trash" as a child, was raised in poverty in a bad neighborhood. What drove him, above all else, was a desperate need to provide a better childhood for his own kids. This was the most important part of his story.

Soon after he shared his story, this very shy man was approached by genuinely interested people who felt connected to him on a deeper level. He left that day with more friends than he came in with. That's the power of authentic storytelling.

Being authentic means tapping into your values. Authenticity is what makes it possible for you to build the relationships you need to get unstuck, unburdened, and to become unstoppable!

:: STEP 2:
KNOW YOUR VALUES

Peter Thomas, the author of the book Be Great, said that there are two ways to be happy: to do things that match your values, or to change your values. Values are notoriously hard to change, of course, because we feel them on a gut level. So it probably makes more sense to figure out *what* your core values are, and then to stick by them.

Not only will this make you happier, but as you find mentors, you will find that people would much rather help others who share their values. A values-based relationship can be extremely powerful for both people. Most of my mentors have shared my values of service, integrity and family. So what are your core values? Integrity? Service? Humility? Happiness? Fitness?

What are the ideals you most believe in? Whatever they are, spending some time answering this question will set you apart from many of your peers—and it will help you formulate and articulate your own goals more easily.

What are your top three values?

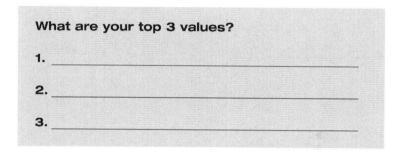

:: **STEP 3:**
CREATE YOUR 30-SECOND COMMERCIAL

Now that you have a list of your values in hand, what is your vision for your life? Are you an ambassador of goodwill? Are you an accomplished business person who adds value? Are you someone who pushes the limit in whatever you do? Your vision statement should be a 30-second commercial, or a few sentences long, and it should capture *who* you want to be, your core values, what you want to do, and why you want to do it.

My friend Patricia Hudak, founder of RealWorld101.org, has a vision of "saving her generation 'from a lower quality of life by giving them the life-skills education they never learned in college.'" This matters to her because, as she puts it, she graduated from a good school with a ton of student loan debt and was unprepared for the real world. She values making life easier for others.

People hear her story and instantly connect. The same can be true of your story, when it's articulated in a clear vision statement. For a free detailed "life exercise" to help you discover your vision, visit the resources pages at the back of this book.

:: WRITING EMAILS
THAT DON'T GET DELETED

Here is an example of a real attention-grabbing email someone sent me with a great "story":

Hi Bert,

"I hope this message finds you well. I was introduced to you on Facebook by my friend Maria. I would like to verify if you have any time to meet this week. Your passion for mentorship and career achievements impress me a lot. As I see you were also a SIFE member. I was a project leader and we presented at a SIFE regional competition. I have a great desire to learn and to give back to the community. That is why a Meetup for Women in IT was created. But I lack experience in the area of organizing forums and events. I have made small steps to build out the Women in IT community and I would really appreciate your help.:

Thank you,

I was sold on on this person as soon as I read her email. She not only linked us through an organization we both cared about (Students in Free Enterprise, SIFE) we also connected on a shared value, her desire to give back to the community (service), and it became my priority to respond to her. The more you connect with someone with your story and your values, the more they will want to go above and beyond for you.

:: PUTTING IT ALL TOGETHER

Now that you have followed the three steps to create your story, you have to publicize your story and share it. A great strategy is to put up a one-page website and add it to your email signature. www.Wix.com and www.weebly.com are two places you can go to build a free website without any prior programming knowledge.

Call five of your closest friends and ask them, "What do I do better than anyone else?"

Answer the questions below to create the building blocks for your story.

Who do I want to be? (What are three things they may write about me on my tombstone?)What are my values?

Want the secret to deeply satisfying career success? Focus on the parts of your job that tie into your values, who you want to be, what you do better than anyone else, and your story.

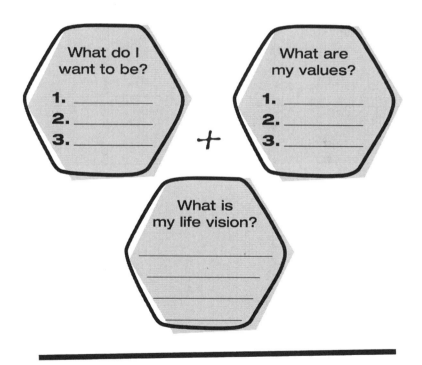

What do I do better
than anyone else?

What do I
want to be?

1. _____
2. _____
3. _____

+

What are
my values?

1. _____
2. _____
3. _____

What is
my life vision?

_____
_____
_____
_____

= My Story :)

Chapter Nine

Chapter Ten:

Type:

What Types Of People Should You Approach To Mentor You?

So now you know *who* you are, and you've got that compelling story to share, chock-full of your own most deeply held values. You're ready to attract the right mentor.

But who is that, and what does this person look like? Who should you approach to be your mentor? Should your mentor be someone older than you, or closer to your age? Does your mentor *have* to be someone in a high-level position, like a manager? Should this person work where you work?

You'll ask yourself all of these questions, and the truth is, there is no one right answer. In fact, you will eventually find that there are different types of people who fit the bill at different times in your career. But finding your first mentor doesn't have to be difficult. Here are some simple rules to help you make sense of it all.

:: YOU CAN'T FEED STEAK
TO A BABY

The popular phrase "You can't feed steak to a baby" contains a warning: don't bite off more than you can chew. When you're out there, attracting successful mentors, there is a certain natural order to the process. And if you ignore it, you risk winding up frustrated and disillusioned.

Let's put it this way: You wouldn't want your first basketball coach to be LeBron James. That would be intense. You would probably end up thinking he was crazy for making you run up a mountain dribbling a basketball blindfolded. Eventually, you would become frustrated by his unrealistic expectations and frustrated with yourself for letting him down—and you would probably never want to play the sport again. A good high school coach, on the other hand, could jump-start a career as illustrious as LeBron's—without the pressure.

This is probably the number one mistake people make when looking for a mentor early in their careers. They go too high up, before they're really ready. In other words, they try to feed steak to the baby.

Let's look at a chart of the different types of career profiles you may run into when first attracting mentors, so we can figure out how to navigate these profiles. A great low-pressure way to get started is to find a mentor from the professional chart below who has the right experience to help you on one specific, short-term, measurable outcome. Focusing on a short-term goal first can help you figure out where to go next.

Newbees — These are first or second-year professionals. These people are great to exchange knowledge and expertise with about specific parts of easing into your job. In particular, they make great hosts and can be part of your support network during those crucial first three months on the job.

Up-and-Comers — People who are still relatively new to an industry but have been around long enough to make a name for themselves are the Up-and-Comers. These are the folks who will probably be the most empathetic to your struggles, because they just went through them. They have been around a few years and probably have a few connections and introductions they can make to help you. But because of their ambition, role, and the reality that they might be starting families at this point in their career, be aware that these people may have limited time.

Established Professionals — With 10 or more years experience in one specific industry, these professionals can help you find direction—and they can help you look at an aerial view of your career. Established professionals are good mentors because they are usually a little older than you, settled down, and not in direct competition for the opportunities you are pursuing. Their perspective can help you better navigate your career and make long-term decisions.

Gurus — Think Yoda. This is someone who is widely recognized as a leader in their industry or field. They have a wealth of information, a vast list of contacts, and can accelerate your career with a single phone call. But there is much more at stake for these people and their hard-earned reputation, so earning their trust will be slow and will take a considerable amount of work. When you start attracting gurus to your hive, you will probably be at the point where you are exceeding even your wildest dreams of success. Gurus are *not* for beginners.

Chapter Ten

:: QUALITIES TO LOOK
FOR IN A MENTOR

Most people get caught up in status, knowledge, age, gender, race, and expertise when looking for a mentor. The biggest predictors of success in a mentor relationship, however, are shared values, consistency, and security. If you can't clear the first hurdle of connecting with someone who shares and respects your values, who is secure in their position (won't compete with you for opportunities) and who can make and keep a time commitment, than you might as well be building a house on a sand foundation.

Here are three common missteps people make when looking for the right type of mentors:

1. Preachers who don't practice- We all have a friend, sister, cousin, or uncle who likes to "fake it until they make it." The problem is when they want to teach you "it" before they have created the reality in their own life. Make sure your mentor can speak with credibility and integrity about what they teach you (because she has actually done it).

2. Boss mentors- For many us it is hard to open up to a direct boss and build trust. Without trust you won't have the foundation you need to build a strong mentor relationship.

3. The smart "clique"- Have you ever seen how children draw? Rectangles look like rhombuses, and dragons have feathers. Brilliant! Children don't follow the same rules regarding what people, shapes, or colors are supposed to look like, and as a result they are insanely creative. The minute you stop being a child and listen only to the opinions of one clique (your industry, or executives in your company), your creativity dies. Keep yourself innovative by having a few mentors that are outside of your immediate circle.

:: ACTION STEP
TO GET STARTED!

Start small. Focus on finding one mentor first. Ideally, this person will be a willing up-and-comer or established professional, someone with enough experience to nurture you during a short-term project—think maximum two to four weeks. By working on a project that is short-term, like taking out two people in your industry to lunch, you can produce a small victory for both you and your mentor in a low-pressure environment.

In the resources section, I have included a 30-day action plan detailing how to come up with your short term project and how to get it done with the help of a mentor. If you need help, check it out—and then, take action!

:: IS ONE MENTOR
ENOUGH?

While it's a good idea to start out with one mentor relationship to get a feel for how it works, as we learned earlier in this book, the new reality of the workplace makes these relationships both rare and extremely valuable.

"The advice used to be, 'Go find yourself a mentor,'" Elizabeth Collins writes in her article, "360 Degree Mentoring." "Now the advice is to build a small network of five to six individuals who take an active interest in your professional development."

Eventually, you too will want to create an entire group of mentors, a diverse selection of folks who are around your age, older, younger, and anywhere in between, who can each serve in different roles for you. Just like every bee in the hive adds value in a different way, you too must develop different relationships to sustain harmony and continued success. You must build your hive—and that requires more than one relationship.

Having different types of people in this core group is the foundation of a successful hive. Below are the different types of mentors you should have in your ideal hive, which you'll be continually building as you grow your career:

Mufasa — Do you remember the scene in the Disney movie "The Lion King" when Simba is lost in the wilderness? Out of nowhere, his deceased father, King Mufasa, appears in the clouds to give him advice on how to master the circle of life and get out of the wilderness. In real life, we all could use a Mufasa. Having someone who knows the ropes, who has been exactly where you are and where you want to be, and who can point you in the right direction is crucial to your hive. Mufasas can help you master your circle of life (ahem, career).

Mufasas are the big-picture people you meet with every few months who offer you perspective. We are often so focused on the day-to-day that we can only see what is right in front of us. Mufasas are great because they are able to see your life as a pilot would, from 10,000 feet in the air. From this altitude, they can help you discover your strengths and passions, and ultimately give you good ideas on where to take your career next.

Idea Hawks — If you are an entrepreneur or in a creative field, the "Idea" part will apply to you more so than most. Idea mentors can save you much time and energy by helping you clarify your ideas and focus on the best ones. The "Hawk" part applies to everyone who desires success. Every successful person you know has someone who acts as an "accountability hawk," making sure they do what they say they are going to do.

Super successful people are ruthless about this, and the level of accountability you take on is directly related to the level of success you will enjoy. Idea Hawks can help you zero in on what works—and then get it done!

Supporters — Supporters are the people who are there to help you solve day-to-day challenges in the workplace. These are also the people you vent to. Your friends and people on a similar level in your company make great Supporters.

Spark Plugs — People who actively push you in your career are your Spark Plugs. They will be the ones who make sure you get the visibility you need in a company, get the right projects, meet the right people, and shine in front of the big dogs. Some books call these people "sponsors." It's the same principle: Spark Plugs are usually people who see themselves in you, have a deep investment in your progress, and are willing to give your career a jolt. They have the power and authority to advocate for you and secure opportunities. Always deliver for your Spark Plugs. When you are completely focused on what you want and how to get there, Spark Plugs can be great mentors.

Anthony Pugliese has been one of the top producers at Amway Global for the last 10 years. What's his secret? You guessed it: He credits his enormous success in network marketing squarely on his ability to build a network of trusted mentors, young and old, with varying talents and life experiences. He has successfully built and maintained a hive of mentors; he doesn't go it alone. This is the piece most of us are missing, often without realizing it.

Once you build up your network of Supporters, Mufasas, Spark Plugs and Idea Hawks, you will quickly find yourself in a class above your peers. These people don't all have to work at your company either. That's the beauty of this process: You take an active role in figuring out who you work with best. Once you learn to collaborate, transfer knowledge and share a mutual stake in each other's success, life becomes incredibly easy.

WARNING: If you don't build your network of mentors, it will become increasingly difficult to get the opportunities, expertise and assignments that will advance your career. In other words, you'll stay on the slow track to success—better known as the average way. Diligence and hard work matter, but without the support, guidance and knowledge transfer of an active network, you'll be looking at that three percent raise so many of us settle for, year after year.

The first step to achieving above-average results is to pick one of these "types" of mentors to start with, and then get out there and introduce yourself.

Chapter Ten

:: WHO'S IN YOUR TOP HIVE?

:: HOT TIPS!

Are you still perplexed about how to get started? Having trouble identifying the perfect mentor type to jump-start your hive building? I have a simple exercise that can help.

Go through this simple questionnaire to figure out what your specific area of need is before you approach a potential mentor. This questionnaire was originally posted on www.mindtools.com, and it's a handy way to identify what you need to work on *now*.

Check the ones that apply to you.

❏ Why do I need a mentor?

❏ Do you need a specialist in your field?

❏ Are you looking to improve part of your work performance?

❏ Are you looking to expand into a different career profession?

❏ Are you looking to manage office politics?

❏ Do you need validation that you're headed in the right direction?

❏ Do you need motivation to stretch yourself?

❏ Are you looking for skills to help you get a better job?

❏ Do you need inspiration?

❏ Do I need someone who will help me network with other people in my field?

Chapter Eleven:

Introduction:

How To Introduce Yourself
Like A Champion To Everyone
You Meet Every Time.

:: MENTOR RELATIONSHIPS
ARE LIKE BUILDING BRIDGES

When I was younger I was scared of bridges. I hated them. Anytime we drove anywhere that involved a bridge, my palms itched, my knees trembled, and I would bury my face in my lap. Yet today I drive on bridges without giving them a second thought.

How did I get over this fear? Simple: I built one. Once I learned all the inner workings and techniques involved in building bridges, I realized that they were quite safe. Who knew?

Similarly, once you learn how to build relationships with mentors — and learn to navigate all of the social techniques involved — you will realize that this is no more intimidating than riding a bike or driving on a bridge. Because it's not the bridge that we fear, but the lack of understanding about the bridge. In this chapter, I will walk you through a step-by-step method to introduce yourself to your ideal mentor.

:: FEEL THE FEAR
AND DO IT ANYWAY

Spoiler alert! This is the part where 90 percent of you will quit on me. For most of us, the thought of getting out of our comfort zones and introducing ourselves to someone we admire is about as pleasant as watching paint dry...on cable.

Before you freak out on me, I encourage you to have an open mind. If you're thinking, "This stuff won't work for me, it only works for you Bert, because you're outgoing, and I'm not," then I'm going to let you in on a little secret. What I'm about to say is actually embarrassing for me to share because I've never told anyone about it before, but I think it will help us build the bridge together, so it's worth taking the leap. Here goes!

"How many pennies are in a dollar?" The scratchy teacher's voice echoed in my head. "How many, Bertrand? Berrrtrand!??"

Too embarrassed to speak, I couldn't say a single word. I was suddenly overly aware of my thick Haitian accent, my "differentness," and how foreign I was to my classmates.

"If she asks me that question one more time, I might... no, I will kill her," I thought.

Ten painful minutes of teasing and ridicule and jeers from cruel grade school kids ensued.

The teacher just watched.

Like a cowardly friend who freezes up while the bully punches you in the face, my teacher simply stood by silently as the kids ripped the flesh off of any confidence I had.

To this day, no one in that class knows that I had to go to six months of therapy for social awkwardness. No one knows that one student mailed me a racist hate letter, stripping me of whatever confidence remained. And one thing is for sure... **no one in that class room knows I didn't grow up counting pennies. (In Haiti, we use gourde.)**

I don't have to imagine what it's like to choke up at the thought of speaking to people. I don't have to imagine what it's like to suffer so many let-downs, disappointments and cruelty from others that you could care less if you ever make another friend.

I lived it.

To sweeten the deal, the therapist insisted that my parents be in the room while he asked questions about why I felt like a loser at school.

In other words, friends, I know awkward. I'm Captain Awkward. If I can overcome my fear of speaking to people, you can too—I promise. Let's cross that bridge together.

:: APPROACHING
A MENTOR

Do you have a best friend? Most of us do. But how did this come to be? Did you walk up to her and ask, "Want to be my BFF?" Chances are, your relationship evolved naturally after you discovered mutual interests and values.

Mentor relationships are no different. Your goal when you meet a successful person is to get the next meeting. In most cases, asking someone "Do you want to be my mentor?" after 15 minutes of knowing them sounds awkward. Generally speaking, it's better to talk to and get to know someone before you formalize the relationship, just as it is with any other relationship. ("Will you be my girlfriend?" only works in third grade.)

And don't worry about striking gold the first time around. You may have to meet with several different people before you find the right mentor.

:: GETTING THE MEETING

Once you identify someone who is a potential mentor, a good next step is to invite them to lunch.

How do you do this? Emails are a great first step, especially if the person is busy. But even writing that email can be challenging.

To help you make your next move, I'm going to share with you a specific email I used to get some time with a high profile CEO. The techniques employed in this email can be found in *The Four-Hour Work Week* by Tim Ferris. I simply customized his formula, and it worked like a charm! See the example on the next page, and use it to generate your own custom email. Once you start writing, it's easier than you think.

:: EMAIL SCRIPT

1. **Explanation of subject line:** Your first job is to get your email noticed, and the sweetest word in any language is someone's first name. Use it to grab your recipient's attention instantly. If you are writing to Mike, start your email with "Hi Mike." An even better "attention-grabber" is to refer to a recent accomplishment or article that he/she has been featured in.

2. **Make sure that you use this exact language in your email:** "I have a specific question that should only take 15 or 20 minutes." This is crucial because it communicates two things:

a.   You respect the person's time. Most people never do this because they only think about their own needs. Successful people put a higher value on their time than anyone else, so when you acknowledge this, you instantly set yourself apart.

b.   You have carefully thought through why you are approaching this person. You also know how this person can add value for you—you have a specific question, after all, not a general inquiry. Remember, both of you will leave the meeting with that warm and fuzzy feeling if you have created a clear way for your mentor to add value.

3. **The reason I asked for a phone conversation** in this email and not lunch is because I lived in a different state from Luke. This script will work just fine if you ask for the lunch meeting.

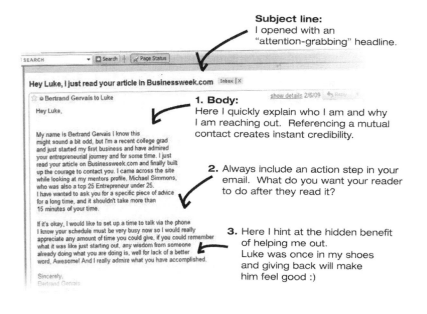

Subject line:
I opened with an "attention-grabbing" headline.

1. Body:
Here I quickly explain who I am and why I am reaching out. Referencing a mutual contact creates instant credibility.

2. Always include an action step in your email. What do you want your reader to do after they read it?

3. Here I hint at the hidden benefit of helping me out. Luke was once in my shoes and giving back will make him feel good :)

Chapter Eleven

:: IN-PERSON SCRIPT

OK, so what if you meet this potential mentor at a conference or a company event? What do you say to set the foundation for a future meeting?

Here is a working script you can use at the end of your conversation, to show that you "get it." Feel free to change it around to fit your personal style. Having a script is good, but you don't want to come off too practiced—tailor it to the conversation, the audience, and your own way of speaking.

> *"It was great talking to you, Christina. I appreciated what you said about the importance of building rapport with your co-workers. I'd like permission to get in touch with you if I have a specific question about what we talked about today."*

After she says yes, be sure to follow up with: "Sounds great. What is the best way to contact you?'"

This simple script does three things:

1. Thanks the person.
2. References valuable wisdom that they shared.
3. Includes an action step. Always ask for permission to follow up if a relevant specific question should come up and establish exactly how you will communicate with one another. Otherwise, you'll have an "in" but no way to use it!

:: PHONE SCRIPT

Let's say you were referred to someone by a mutual contact, so you feel somewhat comfortable and you want to directly ask them to be your mentor.

Here's a great script that I adapted from the book *The Power of Focus: How to Hit Your Business, Personal, And Financial Targets With Absolute Certainty.*   By Jack Canfield, et al.

Hello Kim.

> We haven't met yet. And I know you're a busy woman so I'll be brief. I'm a first-year marketing assistant. In your career you have built both an impressive record of achievement and a stellar reputation.

I'm sure you had some real challenges when you were first starting out. Well, I'm still in those early stages, trying to figure everything out. Kim, I would really appreciate if you would consider being my mentor. All that would mean is spending 15 minutes on the phone with me once a month, so I can ask you a few questions. There is a Starbucks close to your office if you prefer to do it in person. I would really appreciate this, and of course, I will look for ways I could support you, such as attending your book signings and reviewing your work. Would you be open to that?

If they say yes, simply ask to get meeting time sometime in the next few weeks.

If they say no, thank them for their time and ask if they know anyone else who may be interested, have the time and be qualified.

This phone script does three powerful things:

1. Explains exactly what type of mentoring you need.

2. Explains how long the mentoring will be (15 minutes a month) and what it looks like.

3. Offers to add value and sets the tone for a two-way relationship.

For more sample emails and in-person scripts that work, visit my blog www.momentee.tumblr.com.

:: Hot Tip!

Want to know a secret? Most successful people are lonely people who feel unappreciated. Shhhhh... By taking a genuine interest in them or a goal that they accomplished you quickly go from an annoying pest to a welcome guest. That's why referencing an article that they were in, reading their blog, or published work means so much. But this only works when you take a genuine interest in people. That's why step one focused on figuring out your values, interests, and compelling story.

Chapter Eleven

:: **DURING** THE MEETING

After interviewing over 100 successful people for this book, a pattern emerged. There are five things they all did during their meetings to ensure success:

1. **Google:** This is actually a pre-meeting activity, and almost all of my interviewees took this step first. Do some research on the person you are meeting with. Have they accomplished anything recently? Published material? Do they volunteer or champion a cause? Where did they start out? What is going on in their world? These are all great things to know in ad vance.

2. **Take notes:** As soon as he or she starts talking, reach for your notepad and politely ask if you can take a few notes.

3. **Ask for a "trust" challenge:** Every successful person has a book they are reading and it's usually located in their laptop bag. If you picked the right person to have lunch with, then you'll probably want to know what books, blogs and media they follow. You can use this to your advantage by asking for a reading challenge at the end of your meeting. This way, you can end your meeting by saying you would like permission to follow up to discuss the recommended book sometime.

4. **Get a referral:** Remember, the quest to find the best men tors is helped by forming a strong network. The best way to build your network is to end your lunch meeting with the following question:

   "Now that you know what my story is and what I am about, is there anyone else you recommend that I get in touch with?" This powerful question demonstrates your eagerness to succeed, opens you up to someone who may potentially be your mentor in the future, and maximizes your time. Instead of connecting with one person in one hour, you might have created two, three, or even four connections in the same hour.

5.   **Give value:** There are many ways to give. Be a listener.

Every one appreciates an attentive listener. Are your mentors part of a non-profit that needs volunteers? Do they have kids who are looking for fun things to do in the city that they are visiting next week? What are they passionate about? All of these answers will give you clues as to how you can create fu ture value for your mentors.

Another great way to give value is to ask good questions. It is the best gift you can ever give to a mentor who gives you their time. A single good question can show that you put thought into the meeting. Of course, each mentor has something different to offer, so you will have to figure out for yourself the best questions to ask.

To get you started on your own questions, here are the top five killer questions to help you break the ice with your mentor. Use whichever ones speak to you.

1.   Is this where you thought you would end up?

2.   What is one thing that surprised you about your curent position or career path?

3.   Looking back at your career, what would you have done differently?

4.   How does your career use your skills and talents and what projects are you working on that best showcase them?

5.   What professional organizations are you associated with and in what ways?

For more questions such as these, sign up for my free newsletter at www.findsuccessmentors.com. And be sure to use the checklist on the next page after your meeting!

Chapter Eleven

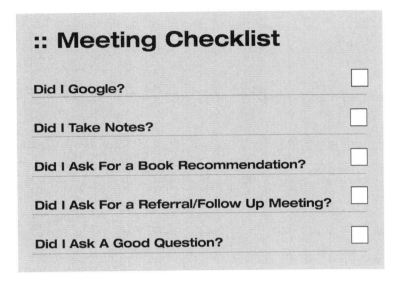

:: **AFTER** THE MEETING

➢ Follow up with a heartfelt, hand-written thank you card.

➢ Follow through on your commitments.

➢ When appropriate, send a follow-up email including points and lessons learned from your conversation.

Chapter Twelve:

Where Do I Find
Great Mentors?

:: **WHERE DO I FIND** MENTORS?

Some of you may be reading this and thinking, "That's great Bert, but *where* do I find these people?" While there's no one right answer, here are a couple of places to start you off—including a few that might surprise you.

Speeches at Colleges:

Colleges are great because they tend to draw top experts for speaking. The good news for you is that these talks are usually free or cheap to attend. Even better news is that speakers at college campuses are usually generous with their time and advice (if they weren't, they wouldn't be there giving a talk or lecture). Use this to your advantage.

> ➤ **Action step:** Google some local people you would be interested in having as mentors. Go on the websites of the colleges nearest you to see if anybody interesting is giving a talk. If they are, prepare ahead: Read up on the person's bio, take notes during their talk, and use the scripts in this chapter to set up a meeting at a later date.

Community Networking:

People like helping people who are like them. There are vast resources on the Internet for communities of people who share your values and your interests. In my opinion, the best resource on the Internet is Meetup.com. Let's say, for example, that you would like to get a mentor in the nursing profession. You can find a meeting or a "meetup" of nursing professionals in your local area.

> ➤ **Action step:** Go to websites like Meetup.com and find a community that represents your industry or core values. Attend one meetup within 30 days and begin to build your network. If the community does not exist, host your own networking event and create the community yourself. No excuses!

Conferences and Associations:

Every industry has conferences, trade shows and associations. These are great places to meet all sorts of professionals who can help you advance in your career, and since they are career-related events, people are more than willing to talk about what they do and how they do it.

> ➢ **Action step:** If you are working at a company already, ask the human resources department or your boss for a list of these conferences. Or, let's say you do not currently have a job and just graduated from college. Google the human resource contacts at five companies you are interested in working at. Email those contacts and ask if they have a list of upcoming conferences that their employees go to or associations their company belongs to, and choose several of these events to attend yourself. Most of these conferences offer deep discounts if you have a student ID card.

Alumni Networks:

I once met a volunteer mentor from Princeton University who revealed a dirty little secret about alumni networks: No one ever calls!

> ➢ Action step: If you went to college and have access to an alumni network, pick up the phone, call the office and tell them what type of mentor you are looking for. You might just make someone's day.

Volunteer:

One way to a successful person's heart is through the charities and causes that he or she believes in. One out of three Americans currently volunteers for a cause, so this is a terrific way to meet people.

> ➢ **Action step:** Research local volunteer opportunities that are of interest to you in your neighborhoods and find out more about their mission and the types of volunteers they attract. Chances are, if an organization's mission appeals to your core values, it will also appeal to future mentors (from Supporters to Gurus).

Formal Mentoring Programs:

Don't make life tougher than it has to be. Just started your first job? Tap into the resources right under your nose. Most larger companies have some type of formal mentoring program.

Chapter Twelve

If being assigned a "formal" mentor isn't your cup of tea, or your workplace doesn't offer a program you're interested in, you can still use the tips in this book to network *within* your company. You can still develop mutually-beneficial relationships and informal mentor networks, with or without the structure of a corporate program.

> ➢ **Action step:** Ask your human resources department representative what programs they currently offer within the company for mentorship, learning and skills training management.

Reverse Mentoring:

This concept, made popular by former General Electric chairman Jack Welch, has started picking up steam. In the pilot version, senior managers at General Electric bartered their experience and know-how with the twenty-something managers in exchange for lessons on becoming more Internet-savvy. Today, we see companies like Bharti, an Indian telecommunications company, using this system to keep their senior managers on top of current trends, music and social media. In turn, these senior managers give younger professionals at Bharti opportunities for experience, growth, and guidance. Find out if such a program exists in your company—or offer to champion it if it does not.

Authors and Professors:

You can perform a Google search on any industry job or profession and find an author, professor, expert or authority in that field. These people are almost always featured in some article or publication. Their name is out there, they're experts, and they're easy to find. Better yet, they're a wealth of industry information.

> ➢ **Action step:** Use the email template in this chapter to get in touch with these folks.

Come back to this page if you ever feel like you've run out of ideas for finding mentors. If none of the ideas listed above work for you, use the extensive list below to generate even more ideas for introductions, or check my website for updates and best practices at www.findsuccessmentors.com.

Chapter Twelve

Relatives	Friends of the family
Friends	Advisors
Neighbors	Fellow classmates
Former employers	Community leaders
Social clubs	Coaches
College professors	Deans
Parents' friends	Alumni associations
Friends' parents	Church leaders
Guidance counselors	High school teachers
Professional	organizations
Industry events	Networking breakfasts
Sorority sisters	Fraternity brothers
Former Employers	Great Networkers

:: 5 Tips For Making
A Great First Impression

Even with all of your careful preparation, you're still shaking in your boots when the moment arrives. What if the mentor doesn't like you? What if the mentor says they don't have time for you? Use my surefire guide to make a great first impression on everyone you meet.

Dr. David Lieberman, an expert on psychology and body language, offers some valuable guidelines on making a great first impression. I've summarized a few of them here for you:

1. **Smile:** When we smile, it accomplishes four powerful things. It demonstrates confidence, happiness and enthusiasm, and — most importantly — it shows acceptance. When we are nervous or uncomfortable, we tend not to smile. Smiling signals confidence and comfort. Not surprisingly, studies show we enjoy being around people who smile.

2. **Establish Rapport:** "Just as we tend to like someone who shares our interests, we are also unconsciously driven to like a person who appears as we do," Dr. Lieberman tells us. The best way to build rapport with someone is to match their

physical behavior. Mirror their body language, breathing patterns, and even phrases they use without being obvious. If they place a hand in a pocket, you follow suit. If they speak slowly, you speak slowly. We tend to like those who make gestures like us so this little tip is a great way to build instant rapport.

3. **Ask to Take Notes.:** This magic phrase will turn a skeptical mentor into an enthusiastic supporter! By asking someone if you can take notes, you subtly communicate two psychological messages. First, you give that person a sense of self-importance, which deep down inside is something we all crave. Second, you show that you are serious, attentive, and willing to learn.

4. **Make Eye Contact:** Most American body language experts agree that making eye contact deepens confidence and builds trust. If you are outside of the United States, you may want to research comparable gestures.

5. **Avoid Saying "I Know":** Most listening books about the topic of listening will tell you that these two little words are a big barrier to good communication. Saying the words "I know" signals the conversation is more about YOU than about the person giving you advice. The trick to listening to people is to make it about THEM. No one enjoys being around a know-it-all.

Nurturing Successful

:: Hot Tip!

Want to know a secret? Most successful people are lonely people who feel unappreciated. Shhhhh... By taking a genuine interest in them or a goal that they accomplished you quickly go from an annoying pest to a welcome guest. That's why referencing an article that they were in, reading their blog, or published work means so much. But this only works when you take a genuine interest in people. That's why step one focused on figuring out your values, interests, and compelling story.

Don't try to impress people. Leadership Professor Angelo Man-strangelo once shared:

:: Hot Tip!

I have been doing this long enough to know when someone is gen-uinely looking for advice or just trying to prove to me how smart they are. Saying 'I know' is a turnoff. You can't come to me trying to show off and expect me to believe you value my advice. That's a bunch of baloney! Sure I'll still help those students because it's my job, but you would be hard-pressed to find a professor that goes above and beyond in that situation. And he shouldn't. Don't miss out on someone going 'above and beyond' for you because you want to prove how smart you are, or even worse, massage your insecurities.

Chapter Thirteen:

Relationships:

How to be a great mentee and nurture mentor relationships that deliver results

Nurturing your relationships will help you to get a lot more value out of them. This is true of friendships and dating, and it's especially true for mentor relationships. The most important factor that determines the success of any relationship is what you do after the initial meeting. The secret to being a great mentee is to treat your mentor like a person and not a stepping stone. If you are proactive, add value, have integrity, and are mindful of your mentor's time, you will do great!

Below, I share five time-tested examples of great relationships.

:: 1. GIVE TO GET

In his book *Do You,* music and fashion mogul Russell Simmons reveals that one of the core rules for success is that "you can never get before you give."

Good mentor relationships are like a two-way highway: Traffic goes in both directions. In this case the "traffic" is the good will, gratitude, care, and knowledge you share. When you decide to give first, you will get back so much more.

Looking beyond your immediate needs isn't just feel-good mumbo jumbo, it's good strategy. Most of your peers are not thinking in this way. When it comes to your hive of mentors, always be thinking about how you can give value. Giving value could mean volunteering at your mentor's fundraiser, being a good listener, having a positive attitude, or just making progress on the things you said you would do. You'll recall from earlier that successful people prosper by practicing enlightened self-interest. Whatever it is, start by focusing on the interests of others and you will be rewarded handsomely.

:: 2. DRIVE THE RELATIONSHIP, ASK FOR WHAT YOU WANT

A guy asks his girlfriend to go to the deli for food. "Pick me up a turkey sandwich the way I like it," he says. When she comes back, to his surprise, the sandwich is on wheat bread (he wanted rye), has

:: **Hot Tip!**

Best selling author Guy Kawasaki recommends that to add value to our network, "*we should eat like a bird and poop like an elephant.*" This simple idea is summarized below.

"Birds eat 50 percent of their body weight per day-and you should do the same when it comes to knowledge of your industry "Once you've become a hub of this information, don't hoard it. Spread it around—like the elephant. Share what you know. Exude dynamism and utility. That way, not only will people circle around you for knowledge and insight, but when they go their merry way, it'll be with your poop on their shoes."

As you learned earlier in the book, we are now in the "knowledge economy" where your ability to transfer and apply information is directly related to how much wealth you create and how many job opportunities you enjoy. So what's the easiest way to give value in a knowledge economy? Become an expert. Whatever your passion is, own it. Be the go to person in your "hive" for this information. By becoming the expert, and sharing that value whenever you can, you become indispensable your relationships.

Free tip: Set up a "google alert" for your "expert" topic and stay ahead of the curve. Whenever you come across an article your mentor would like email it to her.

mustard (he wanted mayo), and contains the wrong cheese!

Feeling frustrated, the boyfriend grumbles, "Thanks, but that's not what I wanted."

Now how do you think that worked out?

One of the biggest reasons we don't get what we want is because we don't ask for exactly what we want. It sounds obvious, and yet many of us fail to make this simple distinction. Not only are we disappointed in the result, but the person who produced the result

Chapter Thirteen

feels disappointed, helpless and frustrated because they couldn't help us in the way they wanted to.

If you want a turkey sandwich on rye, with two pickles, sweet onion dressing and banana peppers, you need to ask for a turkey sandwich on rye with two pickles, sweet onion dressing and banana peppers. Otherwise, don't complain when you get turkey and Swiss on wheat.

Communicating what you want is an important part of nurturing your relationships. When you are specific in what you want, you get more value, and you also help your mentor feel needed and valuable. Nurturing relationships is a win-win.

Here's an example of how better communication gets results:

Example 1:

"Hey Jan, I feel stuck in my career as marketing assistant. I want to get ahead, what do you think I should do?"

Example 2:

"Hey Jan, could you describe to me which skill sets, relationships, and types of projects I would need under my belt to be considered a high-potential candidate for category manager in the next two years?"

Which approach do you think got a more satisfying response that more closely matched what the mentee was looking for?

Asking for what you want also means you have to drive the relationship. Remember, the best mentors are busy people. You can't wait for them to figure out what you need or how to help you. You have to be proactive, set the agenda, ask to get on their calendar, and set up meetings.

SETTING GOALS

Asking for what you want also includes setting goals with your mentors. Be clear in how your mentors can help you by meeting weekly or monthly, and monitor your progress on specific goals. For a guide on setting goals, refer to the resource page in the back of this book.

:: 3. BE HONEST...
REALLY HONEST

KEEP IT REAL

I once reached out to a prominent internet marketing guru for advice on my online business. I felt so intimidated by his success I decided to *slightly* inflate the amount of registered users we had to "impress him." For some reason, I thought he'd discredit me if I didn't measure up to his success.

Nothing could be further from the truth. First of all, anyone worth his salt should be able to detect when someone is putting up a front. Secondly, if I go to the doctor to get treated for a bruise when I really have a broken leg, I'll get an ice pack when what I really needed was a cast! Sure, I'll keep my pride, but I won't stop limping anytime soon.

Around those you really respect, you may be tempted from time to time to "flub" your accomplishments. Whenever you feel this way, you should take an immediate step back. Overcome your need to impress your mentor or show that you are on the same "level." Being honest about your challenges and shortcomings gives your mentor the best opportunity to help you – and they'll certainly appreciate your honesty. Vulnerability is the building block of great relationships.

KEEP PEOPLE IN THE LOOP

Jazz guitarist Russell Malone says, "When you are not appearing, you are disappearing." Never go into hiding, even when things are not working out. Being up-front with people and acknowledging that you are in a rut, or having a rough time, will always have a higher payoff than avoiding them when things go badly for you.

REPLY BACK WHEN THINGS DON'T WORK OUT

If someone sets up an email introduction for you with one of their contacts, and it doesn't work out, for whatever reason, you should let them know. For example, "Hey Jan, remember that graphic designer you hooked me up with last month? It didn't work out, but thanks again." A short and simple note will demonstrate in a real way to your friend or mentor that you are grateful for their help. Very few people do this and take it for granted that the mentor will just "know." Wrong! It's your job to follow up.

IT'S OK TO LET PEOPLE KNOW THAT YOU DIDN'T TAKE THEIR ADVICE

Parnell Pierre-Louis, a marketing specialist who consults with startups, shared with me his first experience with a mentor. His mentor told him about a job opportunity that she said would be "perfect for him." He tried the job and hated it. Eventually, he quit and went in a completely different direction. Months went by before he mustered up the courage to tell her the truth. Much to his surprise, she wasn't disappointed, or left sulking with a wounded ego. She was thrilled that he had found something he was happy with and thanked him for his honesty.

:: 4. GIVE PRAISE

When was the last time you received a sincere compliment? How did it make you feel? You probably felt like a million bucks. Receiving a heartfelt praise with no ulterior motives is one of the best gifts we can ever receive. The next time you get a chance, think of something you can specifically admire about someone in your network and tell this person immediately.

And the next time you feel frustrated in any mentor relationship, refer back to this check list to see if you have been nurturing the relationship:

:: ARE YOU NURTURING YOUR MENTOR RELATIONSHIPS?

Am I Giving Before I Get? ☐

Am I Asking For What I Want? ☐

Am I Being Honest? ☐

Am I Giving Praise? ☐

:: Tip From The Mentor Guy!
3 Ways To Become Your Mentor's Version of American Idol.

How would you like to have been the person who invented American Idol? Most people want to be part of something larger than themselves, to say "I was there first, and believed!" This principle applies to helping people too. People who invest in you want to know that you're the next big thing. How can you be your mentor's American Idol? Follow these three steps and you'll be singing songs about all the new attention you're getting.

Chapter Thirteen

1. Be Aligned

Quiana Hart was a new analyst on Wall Street at the tender age of 21. She was a southern small town girl eager to prove herself in the heart of the financial world, New York City. Desperate to hit the ground running and keep up with her Ivy League counterparts, she sought out possible mentors who could make a difference in her career. This would not be easy. At her firm most mentors had 10 or so mentees demanding their time. So what did Quiana do? Stand out. She found out that her mentor, Jacques-Philippe Piverger, a principal investor on Wall Street, was also a generous philanthropist who fundraised often for various causes. When Quiana found out about his huge campaign fundraiser for Barack Obama, she knew that she could not give to the cause financially, nor could she give with potential donors. What she did have were two valuable assets she could be generous with-time and energy. She addressed a need by providing Jacques with volunteers who were young like her and still wanted to participate in the campaign. She earned his trust by successfully organizing and managing over 40 volunteers, day-to-day operations, and social media activities for the event. By aligning herself with the causes her mentor valued most, she cultivated a stronger relationship with him and secured more of his time. Remember Quiana's story the next time you want the attention of a mentor.

2. Be Committed

Dweynie Paul was just starting a position at a competitive law firm. She didn't have many connections or feel confident enough to approach people in the office. Her approach to work, however, was unwaivering. First in the office, last to leave was her motto. Her diligence was soon noticed by Jacques Leandre, a senior lawyer who admired her quite confidence. He took her under his wing and has served as her mentor for over one year.

3. Progress Post-Card

In my blackberry I have a file for every person I meet that gives me an idea. Every last one gets noted. Whenever I execute on one of these ideas, I send out a post card with my picture on the front, and on the back I have their idea, the action step I took, and a note of gratitude for the result. This is a killer idea!

Chapter Thirteen

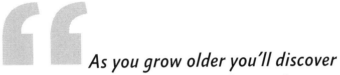

As you grow older you'll discover you have two hands, one for helping yourself, the other for helping others.

-**Audrey Hepburn**

Chapter fourteen:

Nurturing Successful Relationships:

How to be a great mentee and nurture mentor relationships that deliver results

Several years ago, much to the shock of her millions of fans, Oprah stopped promoting her book club. For those of you unaware of Oprah's influence, she was the equivalent of pop dynamite. Any book she promoted blew up. No-name authors reaped orders for millions of books the day after appearing on her show.

Yet one day, amidst all the lives that were being transformed and enhanced, and the demands from millions of fans who waited for the next Oprah endorsement, she pulled the plug. Do you know why? No one ever sent her a thank you card.

We don't have to wait until we lose something to be grateful. We can start with gratitude.

:: ARE WE TOO BUSY
TO BE GRATEFUL?

George Carlin once observed:

> *"The paradox of our time in history is that we have taller buildings, but shorter tempers; wider freeways, but narrower viewpoints; we spend more, but have less; we buy more, but enjoy it less. We have multiplied our possessions, but reduced our values. We talk too much, love too seldom, and hate too often. We've learned how to make a living, but not a life; we've added years to life, not life to years."*

Truer words have never been uttered. So what gives? Pound for pound, we are the wealthiest generation in the history of mankind. Yet unhappiness is rampant. Next time you feel frustrated, down, or insecure, take a moment to reflect on the parts of your life you are grateful for. Write them down. Reflect.

Ironically, it is only when we become grateful for what we do have that we are able to attract abundance to our life.

Chapter Fourteen

:: SO START WITH GRATITUDE

Common sense tells us that being gracious makes us infinitely more likeable. Gracious people tend to over-perform because they are generally happier and don't mind doing the extra nice gesture. Besides, no one likes an ungrateful grouch. Unfortunately, some people are ungrateful without even realizing it. Human nature dictates that we don't always appreciate what we take for granted. *But I'm so busy, when do I have time to appreciate people?*

I get it. When you're trying to make a name for yourself in the beginning of your career, chances are you will probably be feeling swamped. It is hard to even find the time to reflect and appreciate the relationships you do have. We've all been there.

If you find yourself annoyed by the prospect of writing thank you cards, or you keep forgetting to thank people at all, it doesn't mean you are a bad person. It just means you need to practice. Yes! Gratitude can be learned. Here's how:

THANK YOU CARD TUESDAYS

At a seminar in Chicago, Ivanka Trump shared with me a powerful habit. Every week she sends a letter to someone who inspires her, from mega-moguls to shoeshine boys.

Every week. Ivanka Trump. Yes, you read that correctly.
If someone who is supposedly so "well-off" can still find time to be gracious, we all can do the same. Every Tuesday since that seminar, I have been sending at least one thank you card to friends, mentors, and people that I appreciate. Surprisingly, I never run out of names, no matter how many I send.

If you need some inspiration to tap into your gratitude check out the blog www.gratuityinc.com.

*Think of three people
you are grateful for
and get their
addresses tonight!*

Name	Address
1.	
2.	
3.	

Chapter Fourteen

GRATITUDE LIST

Make a list of the top five things you are grateful for. Make sure you stick it somewhere, like your bathroom mirror, where you will see it every day. What are you grateful for? Freedom? The ability to pursue your dreams? Being able to work? Your family? TiVo?

Top 5 things
I am thankful for:

1. _____

2. _____

3. _____

4. _____

5. _____

And that concludes your five steps. You made it! Follow the 30-day plan at the end of this book, and you should be well on your way to not only finding mentors, but exploding to above-average success in your career—with the help of a busy hive of people supporting you every step of the way.

Chapter Fourteen

Chapter Fifteen:

Who's In Your Top Hive?

While writing this book, the most inspiring achievement I came across had nothing to do with business. To be sure, I interviewed my fair share of twenty-something millionaires, CEOs and managers who managed people twice their age, but all of their stories pale in comparison to what my friend shared with me one day.

A few weeks before her third birthday, Bea Fields' daughter was diagnosed with leukemia. It was devastating news. The illness of a child is tough on any parent, but observing life-threatening spinal taps and bone marrow sessions for your three-year-old daughter is "a "crushing blow to my soul," as Fields' revealed. "Six months felt like six years. I really wanted to stay to myself."

There was no support system for mothers dealing with infants with this disease. Months of research and pouring through books and articles on the disease did little to ease the anxiety.

Luckily, one brave doctor had something else in mind. Six months into the treatment for her daughter, which had been yielding only modest results, he came up with a crazy plan. The doctor called Bea and told her that as part of a new initiative, North Carolina State University was looking to start support groups for families with newly diagnosed infants. The doctor even had another mom going through the same episode Bea had gone through just six months earlier.

"The mom is the same age as you," the doctor reported, "and her daughter is the same age as your daughter. You two have a lot in common and should support each other."

"I was reluctant at first," Bea admitted. "As you can imagine, it was such a stressful time, and focusing on being a friend to a stranger was the least of my concerns." Out of a favor to the doctor, Bea called this the woman.

"It was one of the best decisions of my life. We developed a strong bond. We collaborated, shared experiences, coping strategies, and knowledge about how to deal with the disease. Through my experience she saw a light at the end of the tunnel for her daughter." Bea later revealed to me that she still has a relationship with that mother.

Miraculously, both children, who became childhood friends and often played with each other, survived. They are still in touch today.

Chapter Fifteen

Soon enough, the doctor became convinced that these support groups improved medical results. It was almost as if satisfying a deeper social need was impacting the biology of the patients. He realized that if he could build these support networks — the hives — for the families of his patients, based on mutual support, shared knowledge, and experience about dealing with leukemia – then everyone would benefit enormously.

After hearing this story, I wondered, What would be the impact on human potential if we stopped going it alone and formed these support networks? What would happen if we committed to nurturing our mentor networks, our top hives, not just to achieve career success but to elevate our potential as human beings?

If you learned nothing else from this book, remember this: Relationships matter. People matter. And it is only when we realize each other's worth that we find a way to matter to the world.

Thank you for reading.

P.S. When I asked Bea what her daughter, that courageous three-year-old who once braved leukemia, was doing now, she replied, "She's in college, where she chairs the mentoring program for disabled kids at UNC State."

Chapter Fifteen

Mentee Action Guide
8 Steps to Maximize What You Learned in This Book

1. What growth area could a mentor support you with?

- ☐ Inspiration to push your self
- ☐ Job shadowing to learn your industry
- ☐ Improving a specific skill
- ☐ Networking to build industry contacts
- ☐ Strategies to expand your business
- ☐ Other

- ☐ Sounding board for ideas
- ☐ Accountability for major goals
- ☐ Reviewing your resume
- ☐ Grooming you for a leadership role
- ☐ Living a balanced lifestyle
- ☐ Improving part of your work performance

2. Choose a short term project in your growth area.

(For example, If your growth area is to build your industry contacts, a good short term project would entail working with a mentor to set up two lunches with industry contacts in the next 30 days)

3. How much time will you require from your mentor? Check all that apply.

I need to ☐ Email ☐ Call ☐ Meet My Mentor _____
hours per ☐ Week ☐ Month

Pick two places where you will start your search to find a great a mentor. Alumni Office Formal Program Industry Events Human Resources Meetup.com Friends, Family Professors Linkedin

4. Draft and send out your mentoring letter. (Refer to Email Scripts in Ch.11)

5. Set up a lunch meeting.

6. Pick a time and date to celebrate.

I will celebrate my success finding a mentor and moving closer to my dreams on _____(date) at_____(place) with_____(the name of one person you would like to be there).

7. Repeat steps 1-6.

8. Do it over. Good luck! Tell me about your journey I want to hear about it :) bert@findsuccessmentors.com.

16 Useful mentoring websites

1. **http://www.studentmentor.org-** Matches college students with mentors in a variety of fields.

2. **www.momentee.tumblr.com-**Offers interviews and tips from mentees about how mentors benefited them.

3. **www.meetup.com-**Find meetups by industry and interest. Great place to make industry contacts and meet mentors.

4. **www.achievement.org-**Provides brief biographies of top achievers in history, great place to find inspirational mentors.

5. **http://www.mentornet.net-** Matches engineering and science students with e-mentors.

6. **http://thementorexchange.org/-**Offers mentor matching, and mentorship for women in a variety of professions.

7. **www.medicalmentor.org-**Offers resources and mentoring to aspiring health professionals.

8. **www.gottamentor.com-** Offers Q&A with mentors in various fields.

9. **www.jobshadow.com-** Offers transcripts of jobshadow interviews with professionals in various fields. Great way to brush up on your industry before an interview.

10. **www.micromentor.org-**Offers mentor matching, articles, and resources for small business owners.

11. **http://www.ed2010.com-**Great mentor resource for those interested in the publishing and magazine industry. Offers top notch 60- minute mentoring sessions.

12. **www.thecompletelawyer.com-**Offers articles and tips on navigating a law career. Has good advice for finding mentors and sponsors.

13. **www.under30ceo.com-**Great resource for articles, tips, and networking advice for young entrepreneurs.

14. **http://www.mindtools.com**-Great website for developing career skills. Download their useful tools.

15. **www.mentoring.org**- Great site to find local opportunities to be a mentor.

16. **http://careersoutthere.com**- Great resource for video interviews of professionals in a variety fields including healthcare, finance, advertising and public relations.

Interested in being a mentor and volunteering?
Here are four great organizations

1. Year Up **www.Yearup.org**

2. New York Needs You
   http://www.newyorkneedsyou.org/

3. iMentor **http://www.imentor.org/**

4. National Cares Mentoring Movement
   http://www.caresmentoring.org/

I will be updating this list on a consistent basis. For a list of more mentor websites for different industries and more ideas for places to look for mentors go to http://findsuccessmentors.com/resources

FREE

The Mentor Guy

www.**FindSuccessMentors**.com

Do You Want

A College and Diversity Speaker who can inspire, inform, and incorporate your event outcomes in one talk?

Bert is just the speaker for your organization.

Bert Gervais a.k.a Mentor Guy, is one of America's premier speakers for college students, diversity programs, and young professionals. He has been featured on Blackenterprise.com, USA Today, Fox News, and was recognized by President Obama for his work with young America. Bert is an expert on student leadership and success, mentorship, and diversity. To learn more about his speaking topics visit http://findsuccessmentors.com/speaking/

How to contact me:
Phone: 607-206-9589
Email: Bert@FindSuccessMentors.com
www.Facebook.com/TopHive

Notes:

Notes:

Notes:

Notes: